To Jam & Marty
from Otto Jr.
Christmas 1982

Crown's Book of
Political Quotations

Crown's Book of Political Quotations

Over 2500 Lively Quotes from Plato to Reagan

by Michael Jackman

CROWN PUBLISHERS, INC.
NEW YORK

to mom and dad

Inquiries should be addressed to Crown Publishers, Inc., One Park Avenue, New York, New York 10016

Printed in the United States of America

Published simultaneously in Canada by General Publishing Company Limited

Library of Congress Cataloging in Publication Data
Main entry under title:

Crown's book of political quotations.

  Includes indexes.
  1. Political science—Quotations, maxims, etc.
I. Jackman, Mike. II. Crown Publishers.
PN6084.P6C7 1982   081   82-5015
ISBN: 0-517-547376   AACR2

Design by Joanna Nelson

10 9 8 7 6 5 4 3 2 1

First Edition

*In our age there is no such thing
as "keeping out of politics."
All issues are political issues. . .*

George Orwell

Contents

Introduction

If politics is a dirty word, this is an uncensored collection of obscene comments. Most people feel "you cannot adopt politics as a profession and remain honest." [1] As a result, say some folks, "political history is far too criminal a subject to be a fit thing to teach children." [2] Or adults.

But "man is by nature a political animal." [3] "In our age there is no such thing as 'keeping out of politics.' All issues are political issues." [4]

"Government is too big and important to be left to the politicians," [5] but our fashionable reluctance to appear involved has permitted "public office [to be] the last refuge of the incompetent." [6]

We aren't stuck with this condition, however. Perhaps a day will come when politics will once again be acceptable dinner-table talk. And for those who have nothing to say, this collection of slogans should prove useful.

"Democracy will not be salvaged by men who talk fluently, debate forcefully, and quote aptly," [7] but "it is a good thing for an uneducated man to read books of quotations," [8] beginning, of course, with this one. Politics requires a sense of humor to maintain a sense of sanity, and "next to being witty yourself, the best thing is being able to quote another's wit." [9]

The quotes in this book have been selected, using acceptable experimental methodology, because they are entertaining or informative. I have taken responsibility for compiling these quotes despite the fact that "one must be a wise reader to quote wisely and well." [10]

The value of any collection of quotes depends on our relative inability to commit to memory those golden words that only sound significant ten years later. When my memory is hazy, "I quote myself." [11] Besides, "the difference between my quotes and those of the next man is that I leave out the inverted commas." [12]

[1] Louis McHenry Howe.

[2] W. H. Auden.

[3] Aristotle.

[4] George Orwell.

[5] Chester Bowles.

[6] Boies Penrose.

[7] Lancelot Hogben.

[8] Winston Churchill.

[9] Christian N. Bovee.

[10] A. Bronson Alcott.

[11] George Bernard Shaw.

[12] George Moore.

How to Use This Book

The following quotations are listed under category headings that are arranged in alphabetical order.

To locate a subject area that is *not* a category heading, refer to the Subject Index in the back of the book.

An Authors Index, with biographical notations, is also provided in the back of the book.

Category Headings

Crown's Book of
Political Quotations

Advertising

Advertising has done more to cause the social unrest of the 20th century than any other single factor.

Clare Boothe Luce

You can tell the ideals of a nation by its advertisements.

Norman Douglas

The big print giveth and the small print taketh away.

Tom Waitts

Advertising is found in societies which have passed the point of satisfying the basic animal needs.

Marion Harper, Jr.

One-third of the people in the United States promote, while the other two-thirds provide.

Will Rogers

You know why Madison Avenue advertising has never done well in Harlem? We're not the only ones who know what it means to be Brand X.

Dick Gregory

Few people at the beginning of the nineteenth century needed an adman to tell them what they wanted.

John Kenneth Galbraith

Advertising may be described as the science of arresting the human intelligence long enough to get money from it.

Stephen Leacock

Advertising is a valuable economic factor because it is the cheapest way of selling goods, particularly if the goods are worthless.

Sinclair Lewis

To gain, teacheth how to spend.

George Herbert

Advertising is legalized lying.

H. G. Wells

In the factory we make cosmetics; in the drugstore we sell hope.

Charles Revson

It used to be that people needed products to survive. Now products need people to survive.

Nicholas Johnson

Advertising is eighty-five percent confusion and fifteen percent commission.

Fred Allen

Promise, large promise, is the soul of an advertisement.

Samuel Johnson

Business today consists in persuading crowds.

Gerald Lee

Advertising is a racket . . . Its constructive contribution to humanity is exactly minus zero.

F. Scott Fitzgerald

Agriculture

Whoever controls food exports controls the world.

Jacques Chonchol

The farmer is the only man in our economy who buys everything he buys at retail, sells everything he sells at wholesale, and pays the freight both ways.

John F. Kennedy

Grain is the currency of currencies.

Nikolai Lenin

Nobody is qualified to become a statesman who is entirely ignorant of the problem of wheat.

Socrates

Food distribution is not the solution to hunger. The solution lies rather in a redistribution of control over food-producing resources.

Frances Moore Lappé and Joseph Collins

Kansas had better stop raising corn and begin raising hell.

Mary Elizabeth Lease

I've never known a country to be starved into democracy.

George D. Aiken

The nation that destroys its soil destroys itself.

Franklin D. Roosevelt

The accounts of the United States ought to be and may be made, as

simple as those of a common farmer, and capable of being understood by common farmers.

Thomas Jefferson

Dig tunnels deep, store grain everywhere, and never seek hege-
mony.

Mao Zedong

A police state finds it cannot command grain to grow.

John F. Kennedy

The first receipt to farm well is to be rich.

Sydney Smith

No occupation is so delightful to me as the culture of the earth.

Thomas Jefferson

Population, when unchecked, increases in a geometrical ratio. Sub-
sistence only increases in an arithmetical ratio.

Thomas Malthus

Cotton is King.

David Christy

The farmer is covetous of his dollar, and with reason.

Ralph Waldo Emerson

Let us not forget that the cultivation of the earth is the most important labor of man.

Daniel Webster

They that die by famine die by inches.

Matthew Henry

Some people are going to have to starve. . . . We're in the position of
a family that owns a litter of puppies: we've got to decide which
ones to drown.

U.S. Secretary of Agriculture, 1946

No one hates his job so heartily as a farmer.

H. L. Mencken

The agricultural population, says Cato, produces the bravest men, the most valiant soldiers, and a class of citizens the least given of all to evil designs.

Pliny the Elder

The chief problem of lower-income farmers is poverty.

Nelson Rockefeller

America

Ours is a country deliberately founded on a good idea.

John Gunther

I tremble for my country when I reflect that God is just.

Thomas Jefferson

America is a mistake, a giant mistake.

Sigmund Freud

Americans: People who laugh at . . . African witch doctors and spend 100 million dollars on fake reducing systems.

Leonard Louis Levinson

. . . the terrible newly imported American doctrine that everyone ought to do something.

Osbert Sitwell

The great advantage of the American is that he has arrived at a state of democracy without having to endure a democratic revolution and that he is born free without having to become so.

Alexis de Tocqueville

It was wonderful to find America, but it would have been more wonderful to miss it.

Mark Twain

You are right in your impression that a number of persons are urging me to come to the United States. But why on earth do you call them my friends?

George Bernard Shaw

Don't get the idea that I'm one of those goddamn radicals. Don't get the idea that I'm knocking the American system.

Al Capone

In America, an hour is forty minutes.

German saying

God will save the good American, and seat him as His right hand on the Golden Throne.

Theodore Dreiser

The organization of American society is an interlocking system of semi-monopolies notoriously venal, an electorate notoriously un-enlightened, misled by mass media notoriously phony.

Paul Goodman

America means opportunity, freedom, power.

Ralph Waldo Emerson

When you are actually in America, America hurts.

D. H. Lawrence

We must be the great arsenal of democracy.

Franklin D. Roosevelt

The American people never carry an umbrella. They prepare to walk in eternal sunshine.

Alfred E. Smith

There are those, I know, who will say that the liberation of human-ity, the freedom of man and mind, is nothing but a dream. They are right. It is the American dream.

Archibald MacLeish

America is a large, friendly dog in a very small room. Everytime it wags its tail, it knocks over a chair.

Arnold Toynbee

Q. If you find so much that is unworthy of reverence in the United States, then why do you live here?
A. Why do men go to zoos?

H. L. Mencken

America is the only nation in history which miraculously has gone directly from barbarism to degeneration without the usual interval of civilization.

Georges Clemenceau

How prophetic L'Enfant was when he laid out Washington as a city that goes around in circles!

John Mason Brown

We must stop talking about the American dream and start listening to the dreams of Americans.

Reubin Askew

I don't see much future for the Americans. . . . Everything about the behavior of America reveals that it's half judaized and the other half negrified. How can one expect a state like that to hold together?

Adolf Hitler

Anarchy

The anarchist denies the right of any government to trench on his individual freedom.

Herbert Spencer

The anarchist and the Christian have the same ancestry.

Friedrich Nietzsche

Government and cooperation are in all things the laws of life; anarchy and competition the laws of death.

John Ruskin

Anarchism is the doctrine that all the affairs of men should be managed by individuals or voluntary associations, and that the State should be abolished.

Benjamin R. Tucker

Aristocracy

Aristocrat: A demokrat with hiz pockets filled.

Henry W. Shaw

We adore titles and heredities in our hearts, and ridicule them with our mouths. This is our democratic privilege.

Mark Twain

Aristocracy is that form of government in which education and discipline are qualifications for suffrage and officeholding.

Aristotle

I am an aristocrat. I love liberty. I hate equality.

John Randolph

Plutocracy lacks all the essential characters of a true aristocracy: a clean tradition, public spirit, honesty, honor, courage—above all, courage.

H. L. Mencken

Aristocracy, n. Government by the best men. . . . Fellows that wear downy hats and clean shirts—guilty of education and suspected of bank accounts.

Ambrose Bierce

Oligarchy: A government resting on a valuation of property, in which the rich have power and the poor man is deprived of it.

Plato

An aristocracy that shirks its leadership is done for. Its only excuse for existence is that it takes the lead.

Alfred North Whitehead

A society without an aristocracy, without an elite minority, is not a society.

José Ortega y Gasset

A democracy, when put to the strain, grows weak, and is supplanted by oligarchy.

Aristotle

Atheism is aristocratic.

Maximilien Robespierre

Assassination

Assassination is the extreme form of censorship.

George Bernard Shaw

You can kill a man but you can't kill an idea.

Medgar Evers

Caesar was a failure. Otherwise he would not have been assassinated.

Napoleon Bonaparte

A President has to expect those things.

Harry S Truman

The ballot is stronger than the bullet.

Abraham Lincoln

Just as I went into politics because Joe died, if anything happened to me tomorrow, Bobby would run for my seat in the Senate. And if Bobby died, our younger brother Teddy would take over for him.

John F. Kennedy

If a sovereign oppresses his people to a great degree, they will rise and cut off his head.

Samuel Johnson

Attempted assassinations are the accidents of kings, just as falling chimneys are the accidents of masons.

Benito Mussolini

Assassination has never changed the history of the world.

Benjamin Disraeli

The blow by which kings fall causes a long bleeding.

Pierre Corneille

Et tu, Brute!

Shakespeare

An absolute monarchy is one in which the sovereign does as he pleases so long as he pleases the assassins.

Ambrose Bierce

I have definitional problems with the word "violence." I don't know what the word "violence" means.

William Colby

Bureaucracy

A bureaucrat is a Democrat who holds some office that a Republican wants.

Alben W. Barkley

I do not rule Russia; ten thousand clerks do.

Nicholas I

The functionaries of every government have propensities to command at will the liberty and property of their constituents.

Thomas Jefferson

Bureaucracy defends the status quo long past the time when the quo has lost its status.

Laurence J. Peter

But it is not the consolidation, or concentration, of powers, but by their distribution that good government is effected.

Thomas Jefferson

The work of internal government has become the task of controlling the thousands of fifth-rate men.

Henry Adams

Government defines the physical aspects of man by means of the Printed Form, so that for every man in the flesh there is an exactly corresponding man on paper.

Jean Giraudoux

The hallmark of our age is the tension between related aspirations and sluggish institutions.

John Gardner

We can lick gravity, but sometimes the paperwork is overwhelming.

Wernher von Braun

Business

The business of America is business.

Calvin Coolidge

The business of government is to keep the government out of business—that is, unless business needs government aid.

Will Rogers

Government in the U.S. today is a senior partner in every business in the country.

Norman Cousins

Corporations cannot commit treason, nor be outlawed, or excommunicated, for they have no souls.

Edward Coke

I am responsible for my actions, but who is responsible for those of General Motors?

Ralph Nader

If the government was as afraid of disturbing the consumer as it is of disturbing business, this would be some democracy.

Kin Hubbard

The masters of the government of the United States are the combined capitalists and manufacturers of the United States.

Woodrow Wilson

The glory of the United States is business.

Wendell Willkie

A man who knows how to make good bargains or finds his money increase in his coffers, thinks presently that he has a good deal of brains and is almost fit to be a statesman.

Jean de La Bruyère

The public be damned.

William H. Vanderbilt

When morality comes up against profit, it is seldom that profit loses.

Shirley Chisholm

No business which depends for existence on paying less than living wages to its workers has any right to continue in this country.

Franklin D. Roosevelt

Money, and not morality, is the principle of commercial nations.

Thomas Jefferson

Corporation, n. An ingenious device for obtaining individual profit without individual responsibility.

Ambrose Bierce

He [the businessman] is the only one who always seeks to make it appear, when he attains the object of his labors, i.e., the making of a great deal of money, that it was not the object of his labors.

H. L. Mencken

A great deal of the so-called government encroachment on the area of business, labor and the professions has been asked for by the people misusing their freedom.

J. Irwin Miller

Nobody talks more of free enterprise and competition and of the best man winning than the man who inherited his father's store or farm.

C. Wright Mills

Nothing is illegal if one hundred businessmen decide to do it.

Andrew Young

Humans must breathe, but corporations must make money.

Alice Embree

Industry is the root of all ugliness.

Oscar Wilde

Banking establishments are more dangerous than standing armies.

Thomas Jefferson

We demand that big business give the people a square deal; in return we must insist that when anyone engaged in big business honestly endeavors to do right he shall himself be given a square deal.

Theodore Roosevelt

In the pre-capitalist stages of society, commerce rules industry. The reverse is true of modern society.

Karl Marx

The modern corporation is a political institution; its purpose is the creation of legitimate power in the industrial sphere.

Peter Drucker

The craft of the merchant is bringing a thing from where it abounds to where it is costly.

Ralph Waldo Emerson

Take the robber corporations and shake them all to Hell.

Granger **newspaper, 1870s**

The businessman dealing with a large political question is really a painful sight. It does seem to me that businessmen, with a few exceptions, are worse when they come to deal with politics than men of any other class.

Henry Cabot Lodge

If business leaders had channeled one tenth of the energy they devoted to fighting this bill [consumer protection] into improving their products and services they would not find themselves in this fix.

James J. Kilpatrick

I niver knew a pollytician to go wrong ontil he's been contaminated by contact with a businessman.

Finley Peter Dunne

Capitalism

Do you know the only thing that gives me pleasure? It's to see my dividends coming in.

John D. Rockefeller

The amassing of wealth is one of the worst species of idolatry, no idol more debasing.

Andrew Carnegie

Accumulation of wealth at one pole is . . . at the same time accumulation of misery, agony of toil, slavery, ignorance, brutality, mental degradation at the opposite pole.

Karl Marx

You know, the only trouble with capitalism is capitalists; they're too damn greedy.

Herbert Hoover

The trouble with the profit system has always been that it was highly unprofitable to most people.

E. B. White

The few who profit by the labor of the masses want to organize the workers into an army which will protect the interests of the capitalists.

Helen Keller

Capitalism has destroyed our belief in any effective power but that of self-interest backed by force.

George Bernard Shaw

Capitalism and altruism are incompatible; they are philosophical opposites; they cannot co-exist in the same man or in the same society.

Ayn Rand

Civilization and profits go hand in hand.

Calvin Coolidge

The genius of our ruling class is that it has kept a majority of the people from ever questioning the inequity of a system where most people drudge along, paying heavy taxes for which they get nothing in return.

Gore Vidal

The real fight today is against inhuman, relentless exercise of capitalistic power. . . . The present struggle in which we are engaged is for social and industrial justice.

Louis D. Brandeis

The growth of a large business is merely a survival of the fittest.

John D. Rockefeller

The forces of a capitalist society, if left unchecked, tend to make the rich richer and the poor poorer.

Jawarharlal Nehru

"Freedom" in capitalist countries exists only for those who possess money and who consequently hold power.

Nikita Khrushchev

Capitalism is itself a crime.

G. K. Chesterton

What is capital? It is what is left over when the primary needs of a society have been satisfied.

Aldous Huxley

If capital an' labor ever do git t'gether it's good night fer th' rest of us.

Kin Hubbard

One of the things capitalism brought into the world was democracy, though I do not think the two are inseparable.

Michael Harrington

Capitalism is not merely the production of commodities; it is essentially the production of surplus value.

Karl Marx

The cure for capitalism's failing would require that a government would have to rise above the interests of one class alone.

Robert L. Heilbroner

Competition is the most extreme expression of that war of all against all which dominates modern middle-class society.

Friedrich Engels

The dynamics of capitalism is postponement of enjoyment to the constantly postponed future.

Norman O. Brown

Censorship

You have not converted a man because you have silenced him.

John Morley

The first thing will be to establish censorship of fiction. Let the censors accept any tale that is good, and reject any that is bad.

Plato

Censorship may be useful for the preservation of morality, but can never be so for its restoration.

Jean Jacques Rousseau

To limit the press is to insult a nation; to prohibit reading of certain books is to declare the inhabitants to be either fools or slaves.

Claude A. Helvétius

You have a right to burn books or destroy books if you can prove that they can do harm.

Thomas Devine

We can never be sure that the opinion we are endeavoring to stifle is a false opinion; and if we are sure, stifling it would be an evil still.

John Stuart Mill

Any country that has sexual censorship will eventually have political censorship.

Kenneth Tynan

The ultimate censorship is the flick of the dial.

Tom Smothers

I never knew a girl who was ruined by a bad book.

Jimmy Walker

Every burned book enlightens the world.

Ralph Waldo Emerson

And since we do not allow improper language, clearly we should also banish pictures or speeches from the stage which are indecent.

Aristotle

All despotisms should be considered problems of mental hygiene, and all support of censorship should be considered as problems of abnormal psychology.

Theodore Schroeder

We all know that books burn—yet we have the greater knowledge that books cannot be killed by fire.

Franklin D. Roosevelt

It is the grossness of the spectator that discovers nothing but grossness in the subject.

William Hazlitt

The liberty of thinking and publishing whatever one likes . . . is the fountainhead of many evils.

Pope Leo XIII

Civil Rights

As a man is said to have a right to his property, he may be equally said to have a property in his rights.

James Madison

The rights you have are the rights given you by this Committee [the House Un-American Activities Committee]. *We* will determine what rights you have and what rights you have not got.

J. Parnell Thomas

The 1964 Civil Rights Act was the best thing that ever happened to the South in my lifetime.

Jimmy Carter

I would have voted against the Civil Rights Act of 1964.

Ronald Reagan

I've voted against them [civil rights]. . . . What you're doing is creating rights at the expense of other people.

Benjamin R. Blackburn

We shall overcome.

Martin Luther King, Jr.

Behind the phrase "law and order" many conceal their opposition to civil rights enforcements and to dissent.

Ramsey Clark

Disobedience, n. The silver lining to the cloud of servitude.

Ambrose Bierce

In any nonviolent campaign there are four basic steps: collection of the facts to determine whether injustices exist, negotiation, self-purification, and direct action.

Martin Luther King, Jr.

Democracy will never solve its problems at the end of a billy club.

Lyndon B. Johnson

I am the inferior of any man whose rights I trample underfoot.

Horace Greeley

It may be true that the law cannot make a man love me, but it can keep him from lynching me, and I think that's pretty important.

Martin Luther King, Jr.

They'll [House Un-American Activities Committee] nail anyone who ever scratched his ass during the National Anthem.

Humphrey Bogart

Communism

The theory of communism may be summed up in one sentence: Abolish all private property.

Karl Marx and Friedrich Engels

What are our schools if not for indoctrination against Communism?

Richard M. Nixon

Any pitcher who throws at a batter and deliberately tries to hit him is a Communist.

Alvin Dark

Eisenhower told me never to trust a Communist.

Lyndon B. Johnson

There are as many communists in the freedom movement as there are Eskimos in Florida.

Martin Luther King, Jr.

Communism is a society where each one works according to his ability and gets according to his needs.

P. J. Proudhon

Leninism is a combination of two things which Europeans have kept for some centuries in different compartments of the soul—religion and business.

John Maynard Keynes

The mind of the universe is communistic.

Marcus Aurelius

The Communist is a Socialist in a violent hurry.

W. Gough

I have in my hand 57 cases of individuals who would appear to be either card-carrying members or certainly loyal to the Communist party, but who, nevertheless, are helping to shape our foreign policy.

Joseph McCarthy

Who was the first around the moon? An atheist Russian or God-fearing American?

Don Carpenter

Communism deprives no man of the power to appropriate the products of society; all that it does is to deprive him of the power to subjugate the labour of others by means of appropriation.

Karl Marx and Friedrich Engels

Neither communism nor anti-communism can be built on mountains of human corpses.

Bertrand Russell

Christian theology is the grandmother of Bolshevism.

Oswald Spengler

Communist: an intensely proud person who proposes to enrich the common fund instead of to sponge on it.

George Bernard Shaw

What is thine is mine, and all of mine is thine.

Plautus

The dictatorship of the Communist Party is maintained by recourse to every form of violence.

Leon Trotsky

Communism and religion are the two trades a fool may succeed at as well as the smartest practical man.

E. W. Howe

In the economic sense, our socialism was more like state capitalism. . . . Marx had never dreamed of anything of the sort. . . . Soviet Russia had broken with everything in her history that was revolutionary, and had got into the usual rails of great-power imperialism.

Svetlana Alliluyeva

Congress

Congress is so strange. A man gets up to speak and says nothing. Nobody listens—and then everybody disagrees.

Boris Marshalov

About all I can say for the United States Senate is that it opens with prayer and closes with an investigation.

Will Rogers

Reader, suppose you were an idiot. And suppose you were a member of Congress. But I repeat myself.

Mark Twain

If the present Congress errs in too much talking, how can it be otherwise in a body to which the people send 150 lawyers?

Thomas Jefferson

They say women talk too much. If you worked in Congress you know that the filibuster was invented by men.

Clare Boothe Luce

Why are congressmen called public servants? You never see servants that anxious to keep their jobs.

Robert Quillen

Ignorance, idleness and vice may be sometimes the only ingredients for qualifying a legislator.

Jonathan Swift

All legislative powers herein granted shall be vested in a Congress of the United States, which shall consist of a Senate and House of Representatives.

Article I, U.S. Constitution, 1790

One of the greatest delusions in the world is the hope that the evils in this world are to be cured by legislation.

Thomas B. Reed

It could probably be shown by facts and figures that there is no distinctly native American criminal class except Congress.

Mark Twain

Congress, n. A body of men who meet to repeal laws.

Ambrose Bierce

Senate, n. A body of elderly gentlemen charged with high duties and misdemeanors.

Ambrose Bierce

Generals should never do anything that needs to be explained to a Senate committee—there is nothing one can explain to a Senate committee.

Harry S Truman

In any assembly the simplest way to stop the transacting of business and split the ranks is to appeal to a principle.

Jacques Barzun

We have the power to do any damn fool thing we want to do, and we seem to do it about every ten minutes.

William Fulbright

The Congress doesn't run—it waltzes.

Charles Joseph

Some statesmen go to Congress and some go to jail. It is the same thing after all.

Eugene Field

I have a new theory—there are no *real* conservatives in Congress.

David Stockman

You can't use tact with a Congressman. A Congressman is a hog. You must take a stick and hit him on the snout.

Henry Adams

Congressmen, because they run for office every two years, are distilled politicians.

Richard Reeves

When a fellow you knew in school attains some lofty public office, you're glad for his sake—but somewhat apprehensive for the future of this country.

Bill Vaughan

Legislation is like sausage—it's a mixture of pleasant and not so pleasant things.

Charles Royer

Conservative

Conservatives are not necessarily stupid, but most stupid people are conservatives.

John Stuart Mill

Some of you may remember that in my early days I was a sort of a bleeding heart liberal. Then I became a man and put away childish ways.

Ronald Reagan

Conservatism defends those coercive arrangements which a still lingering savageness makes requisite.

Herbert Spencer

The modern conservative is engaged in one of man's oldest exercises in moral philosophy, that is the search for a superior moral justification for selfishness. . . . The conspicuously wealthy turn up urging the character-building value of privation for the poor.

John Kenneth Galbraith

A conservative is a man who just thinks and sits, mostly sits.

Woodrow Wilson

The middle of the road is all of the usable surface. The extremes, right and left, are in the gutters.

Dwight D. Eisenhower

The middle of the road is where the white line is—and that's the worst place to drive.

Robert Frost

Some fellows get credit for being conservative when they are only stupid.

Kin Hubbard

Liberalism is trust of the people tempered by prudence; Conservatism is distrust of the people tempered by fear.

William Ewart Gladstone

Conservative, n. A statesman who is enamored of existing evils, as distinguished from the Liberal, who wishes to replace them with others.

Ambrose Bierce

A conservative is a man who does not think that anything should be done for the first time.

Frank Vanderlip

Traditionalists are pessimists about the future and optimists about the past.

Lewis Mumford

The conservative is led by disposition, not unmixed with pecuniary self-interest, to adhere to the familiar and the established.

John Kenneth Galbraith

Conservatism is the worship of dead revolutions.

Clinton Rossiter

The most dangerous thing in the world is to leap a chasm in two jumps.

David Lloyd George

Conservatism is the worship of dead revolutions.

Clinton Rossiter

Conservatism is the maintenance of conventions already in force.

Thorstein Veblen

A conservative is a man with two perfectly good legs who, however, has never learned how to walk forward.

Franklin D. Roosevelt

Conservatism offers no redress for the present and makes no preparation for the future.

Benjamin Disraeli

In most countries, people grow fiercely possessive of their property. It is a bastion of conservatism.

Gordon W. Allport

What is conservatism? Is it not adherence to the old and tried, against the new and untried?

Abraham Lincoln

A liberalism incapable of fiscal self-discipline brought about a radical conservatism conspicuous for its selfishness and insensitivity.

Felix G. Rohatyn

There may be as much biochemical difference between a "schizophrenic" and a "normal" as between a liberal and a conservative, though in the latter case the definitions are sharper and the behavior more predictable.

Hugh Drummond

The radical Right is not so much the enemy of Communism as it is the enemy of freedom.

Frank Church

There is danger in reckless change; but greater danger in blind conservatism.

Henry George

I shall not grow conservative with age.

Elizabeth Cady Stanton

The most conservative persons I ever met are college undergraduates.

Woodrow Wilson

When a nation's young men are conservative, its funeral bell is already rung.

Henry Ward Beecher

Constitution

We don't want nothing but the Constitution, no more, no less.

Dick Gregory

The Constitution not only is, but ought to be, what the judges say it is.

Charles Evans Hughes

All that is valuable in the United States Constitution is one thousand years old.

Wendell Phillips

I'm as conservative as the Constitution, as liberal as Lincoln, and as progressive as Theodore Roosevelt.

George Romney

Your Constitution is all sail and no anchor.

Thomas Macaulay

A good constitution is infinitely better than the best despot.

Thomas Macaulay

I have never been more struck by the good sense and the practical judgment of the Americans than in the manner in which they elude the numberless difficulties resulting from their Federal Constitution.

Alexis de Tocqueville

Corruption

Your President is no crook!

Richard M. Nixon

The illegal we do immediately. The unconstitutional takes a little longer.

Henry Kissinger

The rulers of the State are the only ones who should have the privilege of lying, either at home or abroad; they may be allowed to lie for the good of the State.

Plato

Crime is contagious. If the government becomes a lawbreaker, it breeds contempt for the law.

Louis D. Brandeis

No one can expect the government to act in accordance with the moral code appropriate to the conduct of the individual.

Baruch Spinoza

Those who treat politics and morality apart will never understand the one or the other.

John Morley

They that buy an office must sell anything.

Thomas Fuller

A conscience which has been bought once will be bought twice.

Norbert Wiener

The justification of majority rule in politics is not to be found in its ethical superiority.

Walter Lippmann

I was never worried about any sex investigation in Washington. All the men on my staff can type.

Bella Abzug

I have often been accused of putting my foot in my mouth, but I will never put my hand in your pockets.

Spiro T. Agnew

When I want to buy up any politicians I always find the antimonopolists the most purchasable. They don't come so high.

William H. Vanderbilt

Corruption, the most infallible symptom of constitutional liberty.

Edward Gibbon

An honest politician is one who when he is bought will stay bought.

Simon Cameron

Politics, as the word is commonly understood, are nothing but corruptions.

Plato

The accomplice to the crime of corruption is frequently your own indifference.

Bess Myerson

Few men have virtue to withstand the highest bidder.

George Washington

The more corrupt the state, the more laws.

Tacitus

They who possess the prince possess the laws.

John Dryden

You can't get anything without paying for it.

W. M. Tweed

The purification of politics is an iridescent dream. Government is force.

John James Ingalls

He who exercises government by means of his virtue may be compared to the north polar star, which keeps its place and all the stars turn towards it.

Confucius

The evolutionary process in governments continues. We have passed from Feudalism to Capitalism. Our current stage, as we all know, is Corruption.

Jules Feiffer

Courts

The people can change Congress but only God can change the Supreme Court.

George W. Norris

The courts are not the only instrumentalities of government. They cannot command or regulate the Army.

U.S. Supreme Court, 1911

The decisions of the courts on economic and social questions depend on their economic and social philosophy.

Theodore Roosevelt

There are no more reactionary people in the world than judges.

Nikolai Lenin

Knowing that religion does not furnish grosser bigots than law, I expect little from old judges.

Thomas Jefferson

There is no liberty if the power of judging be not separated from the legislative and executive powers.

C. S. Montesquieu

It is the justice's clerk that makes the justice.

Thomas Fuller

While unconstitutional exercise of power by the executive and legislative branches is subject to judicial restraint, the only check upon our own exercise of power is our own sense of self-restraint.

Harlan F. Stone

I will appoint the first woman to the Supreme Court.

Ronald Reagan

Judges do not answer questions of fact, juries do not answer questions of law.

Edward Coke

The acme of judicial distinction means the ability to look a lawyer straight in the eyes for two hours and not hear a damned word he says.

John Marshall

The judge is condemned when the guilty is acquitted.

Publilius Syrus

There should be many judges, for few will always do the will of few.

Niccolò Machiavelli

Young lawyers attend the courts, not because they have business there but because they have no business anywhere else.

Washington Irving

The thing to fear is not the law but the judge.

Russian saying

Crime

When the President does it, that means it is not illegal.

Richard M. Nixon

When is conduct a crime, and when is a crime not a crime? When Somebody Up There—a monarch, a dictator, a pope, a legislator—so decrees.

Jessica Mitford

Any company executive who overcharges the government more than $5 million will be fined $50 or have to go to traffic court three nights a week.

Art Buchwald

It is no secret that organized crime in America takes in over forty billion dollars a year. This is quite a profitable sum, especially when one considers that the Mafia spends very little for office supplies.

Woody Allen

The streets are safe in Philadelphia, it's only the people who make them unsafe.

Frank Rizzo

People have got so accustomed to having life seasoned with crime and poverty that they cannot contemplate a life without it.

George Bernard Shaw

Poverty is the mother of crime.

Marcus Aurelius

The crime problem is in part an overdue debt that the country must pay for ignoring for decades the conditions that breed lawlessness.

Earl Warren

So long as people, being ill-governed, suffer from hunger, criminals will never disappear.

Kenkò Hoshi

I hate this "crime doesn't pay" stuff. Crime in the U.S. is perhaps one of the biggest businesses in the world today.

Paul Kirk

The desire for "law and order" is nothing so simple as a code word for racism; it is a cry, as things begin to break up, for stability, for stopping history in mid-dissolution.

Garry Wills

The state calls its own violence law, but that of the individual crime.

Max Stirner

Culture

In fact, the chief function of mass culture is to relieve one of the necessity of experiencing one's life directly.

Robert Warshaw

The cultural, if not moral, justification of capitalism has become hedonism, the idea of pleasure as a way of life.

Daniel Bell

Never are the ways of music moved without the greatest political laws being moved.

Aristotle

When I hear anyone talk of culture, I reach for my revolver.

Hanns Johst

Let a hundred flowers bloom. Let a hundred schools of thought contend.

Mao Zedong

Politically I believe in democracy, but culturally, not at all. . . . Whenever a cultural matter rolls up a majority, I know it is wrong.

John Sloan

Without an alternative culture, there can be no alternative press.

Alexander Cockburn

The arts, in general, have need of a king. They glow only under the influence of the scepter. In free states they never shine save when liberty is declining.

Joseph de Maistre

No great art ever yet rose on earth but among a nation of soldiers.

John Ruskin

The men of culture are the true apostles of equality.

Matthew Arnold

Art is the soul of a people.

Romare Bearden

Art upsets, science reassures.

Georges Braque

Democracy

Democracy is simply the bludgeoning of the people, by the people, for the people.

Oscar Wilde

Were there a people of gods, their government would be democratic.

Jean Jacques Rousseau

Democracy substitutes selection by the incompetent many for appointment by the corrupt few.

George Bernard Shaw

Democracy is a form of government by popular ignorance.

Elbert Hubbard

All the ills of democracy can be cured by more democracy.

Alfred E. Smith

As I would not be a slave, so I would not be a master. This expresses my idea of democracy.

Abraham Lincoln

Democracy is a form of government you have to keep for four years no matter what it does.

Will Rogers

Democracy is the worst system devised by the wit of man, except for all the others.

Winston Churchill

Democracy is the recurrent suspicion that more than half of the people are right more than half of the time.

E. B. White

Democracy was invented as a device for reconciling government with liberty.

Bertrand Russell

The republican form of government is the highest type of government: but because of this it requires the highest type of human nature—a type nowhere at present existing.

Herbert Spencer

Democracy is a device that insures we shall be governed no better than we deserve.

George Bernard Shaw

Republic, n. A nation in which, the thing governing and the thing governed being the same, there is only a permitted authority to enforce an optional obedience. . . .

Ambrose Bierce

Government under democracy is thus government by orgy, almost by orgasm.

H. L. Mencken

Democracy is good. I say this because other systems are worse.

Jawaharlal Nehru

Democracy is nothing but a constitutional arbitrary power that has succeeded another constitutional arbitrary power.

P. J. Proudhon

Democracy is based upon the conviction that there are extraordinary possibilities in ordinary people.

Harry Emerson Fosdick

He who would save liberty must put his trust in democracy.

Norman Thomas

In contrast to totalitarianism, democracy can face and live with the truth about itself.

Sidney Hook

A democracy is a government in the hands of men of low birth, no property, and unskilled labor.

Aristotle

Democracy is that form of society, no matter what its political classification, in which every man has a chance and knows that he has it.

James Russell Lowell

. . . that government of the people, by the people, for the people, shall not perish from the earth.

Abraham Lincoln

Democratic Party

If the Republicans will stop telling lies about the Democrats, we will stop telling the truth about them.

Adlai Stevenson

I belong to no organized party—I am a Democrat.

Will Rogers

Republicans sleep in twin beds—some even in separate rooms. That is why there are more Democrats.

William Stanton

You have to have been a Republican to know how good it is to be a Democrat.

Jacqueline Onassis

The Democratic party is like a man riding backward in a carriage. It never sees a thing until it has gone by.

Benjamin Butler

We do not promise what we know cannot be delivered by man, God, or the Democratic party.

Lawrence O'Brien

I never said all Democrats were saloonkeepers. What I said was that all saloonkeepers were Democrats.

Will Rogers

Dictatorship

The more complete the despotism, the more smoothly all things move on the surface.

Elizabeth Cady Stanton

Dictators are rulers who always look good until the last ten minutes.

Jan Masaryk

If our economy of freedom fails to distribute wealth as ably as it has created it, the road to dictatorship will be open to any man who can persuasively promise security to all.

Will and Ariel Durant

Every despot must have one disloyal subject to keep him sane.

George Bernard Shaw

To live by one man's will became the cause of all men's misery.

Richard Hooker

The alternative to the totalitarian state is the cooperative commonwealth.

Norman Thomas

L'état c'est moi.

Louis XIV

No one man can terrorize a whole nation unless we are all his accomplices.

Edward R. Murrow

Despotism violates the moral frontier, as invasion violates the geographical frontier.

Victor Hugo

Force is the vital principle and immediate parent of despotism.

Thomas Jefferson

The danger of social upheaval now may well be universal. . . . I feel building up in this country enormous resentment, mostly political, waiting to be captured.

David Riesman

A dictatorship is a country where they have taken the politics out of politics.

Sam Himmell

The great strength of the totalitarian state is that it forces those who fear it to imitate it.

Adolf Hitler

Diplomacy

Foreign relations is an open book—generally a checkbook.

Will Rogers

A diplomat is a person who can tell you to go to hell in such a way that you actually look forward to the trip.

Caskie Stinnett

Diplomacy—lying in state.

Oliver Herford

I have discovered the art of fooling diplomats: I speak the truth and they never believe me.

Camillo di Cavour

Once the Xerox copier was invented, diplomacy died.

Andrew Young

Diplomacy is the art of saying "Nice doggie!" till you can find a rock.

Wynn Catlin

Foreign ambassadors are nothing but glorified spies.

Napoleon Bonaparte

A sovereign should always regard an ambassador as a spy.

The Hitopadesa, **III, ca. 500**

Diplomats are just as essential to starting a war as soldiers are for finishing it. . . . You take diplomacy out of war, and the thing would fall flat in a week.

Will Rogers

Let us never negotiate out of fear, but let us never fear to negotiate.

John F. Kennedy

A treaty is a promise of a nation.

Fisher Ames

America never lost a war or won a conference.

Will Rogers

Ambassador: a politician who is given a job abroad in order to get him out of the country.

Anonymous

Close alliances with despots are never safe for free states.

Demosthenes

Conferences at the top level are always courteous. Name-calling is left to the foreign ministers.

W. Averell Harriman

Millions for defense, but not one cent for tribute.

Robert Goodloe Harper

In statesmanship get formalities right, never mind about moralities.

Mark Twain

Minister, n. In diplomacy an officer sent into a foreign country as a visible embodiment of his sovereign's hostility.

Ambrose Bierce

Diplomacy today is a collective education in fear.

Alexander von Humboldt

American diplomacy is easy on the brain but hell on the feet.

Charles G. Dawes

Diplomacy is the art of fishing tranquilly in troubled waters.

J. Christopher Herod

A diplomat and a stage magician are the two professions that have a high silk hat. All the tricks that either one of them have are in the hat and are all known to other diplomats and magicians.

Will Rogers

We should consider any attempt [by the European powers] to extend their system to any portion of this hemisphere as dangerous to our peace and safety.

James Monroe

In the field of world policy I would dedicate this nation to the policy of the good neighbor.

Franklin D. Roosevelt

Nobody, not even the most rabid of democrats, can imagine without actual knowledge all the emptiness and quackery that passes for diplomacy.

Otto von Bismarck

Diplomats make it their business to conceal the facts.

Margaret Sanger

In order to be a diplomat one must speak a number of languages, including double-talk.

Carey McWilliams

In politics, as in high finance, duplicity is regarded as a virtue.

Mikhail A. Bakunin

A diplomat's life is made up of three ingredients: protocol, Geritol and alcohol.

Adlai Stevenson

Diplomacy is the art of letting someone else have your way.

Daniele Varè

My advice to any diplomat who wants to have a good press is to have two or three kids and a dog.

Carl Rowan

Diplomacy is to do and say
The nastiest thing in the nicest way.

Isaac Goldberg

Dissent

Congress shall make no law ... abridging ... the right of the people
... to petition the government for redress of grievances.
First Amendment, U.S. Constitution, 1791.

This culture is one of resistance, but a resistance of desperation.
Angela Davis

It is through disobedience that progress has been made, through
disobedience and rebellion.
Oscar Wilde

Insurrection of thought always precedes insurrection of arms.
Wendell Phillips

The most exciting things going on in America today are movements
to change America.
Mario Savio

If our democracy is to flourish, it must have criticism; if our government is to function, it must have dissent.
Henry Steele Commager

Let your motto be resistance, resistance, RESISTANCE! No oppressed
people have ever secured their liberty without resistance.
Henry Highland Garnet

Intelligent discontent is the mainspring of civilization.
Eugene V. Debs

Discussion in America means dissent.

James Thurber

I respect only those who resist me, but I cannot tolerate them.

Charles de Gaulle

Opposition brings discord. Out of discord comes the fairest harmony.

Heraclitus

The heresy of one age becomes the orthodoxy of the next.

Helen Keller

No government can be long secure without a formidable opposition.

Benjamin Disraeli

In my judgment, the war in Vietnam would be over today if we could simply stop the demonstrations in the streets of the United States.

Spiro T. Agnew

Riot, n. A popular entertainment given to the military by innocent bystanders.

Ambrose Bierce

A riot is the language of the unheard.

Martin Luther King, Jr.

Dissent is the journalist's way of asking the scientist's question: "Who says so?" "Can you prove it?" or, simply, "I don't believe it."

Carey McWilliams

The voice of dissent must be heard.

Henry Ford

To disagree with anybody or anything is to run the risk of taking oneself out of the money. All this in a country that was born of controversy. . . .

E. B. White

Draft

The first step in having any successful war is getting people to fight it.

Fran Lebowitz

Every citizen [should] be a soldier. This was the case with the Greeks and Romans, and must be that of every free state.

Thomas Jefferson

In order to have good soldiers, a nation must always be at war.

Napoleon Bonaparte

The functions of a civilian and a soldier are inseparable.

Benito Mussolini

A military force cannot be raised in this manner but by the means of a military force.

Daniel Webster

They talk about conscription as being a democratic institution. Yes; so is a cemetery.

Meyer London

The draft is white people sending black people to fight yellow people to protect the country they stole from red people.

Hair

We are not going to send American boys nine or ten thousand miles away from home to do what Asian boys ought to be doing for themselves.

Lyndon B. Johnson

I'm fed up to the ears with old men dreaming up wars for young men to die in.

George McGovern

No man with gumption wants a woman to fight his nation's battles.

William Westmoreland

One of the problems we're going to have to solve is to make the Armed Forces so popular, everyone wants to get in.

Lewis B. Hershey

Wars will exist until that distant day when the conscientious objector enjoys the same reputation and prestige that the warrior does today.

John F. Kennedy

Older men declare war. But it is youth that must fight and die.

Herbert Hoover

Economics

What we might call, by way of eminence, the dismal science.

Thomas Carlyle

Economists think the poor need them to tell them that they are poor.

Peter Drucker

If all economists were laid end to end, they would not reach a conclusion.

George Bernard Shaw

October. This is one of the peculiarly dangerous months to speculate in stocks in. The others are July, January, September, April, November, May, March, June, December, August and February.

Mark Twain

A study of economics usually reveals that the best time to buy anything is last year.

Marty Allen

The society of money and exploitation has never been charged . . . with assuring the triumph of freedom and justice.

Albert Camus

Whenever there are great strains or changes in the economic system, it tends to generate crackpot theories, which then find their way into the legislative channels.

David Stockman

We are all Keynesians.

Richard M. Nixon

Finance is the art of passing currency from hand to hand until it finally disappears.

Robert W. Sarnoff

The prestige accorded to math has given economics rigor, but alas, also mortis.

Robert Heilbroner

If ignorance paid dividends, most Americans could make a fortune out of what they don't know about economics.

Luther Hodges

If all the nation's economists were laid end to end, they would point in all directions.

Arthur H. Motley

Practical men . . . are usually the slaves of some defunct economist.

John Maynard Keynes

Finance, n. The art or science of managing revenues and resources for the best advantage of the manager. . . .

Ambrose Bierce

In all the recorded history there has not been one economist who has had to worry about where the next meal would come from.

Peter Drucker

One of the greatest pieces of economic wisdom is to know what you do not know.

John Kenneth Galbraith

Nine out of ten economic laws are economic laws only till they are found out.

Robert Lynd

If consumers are asked to make greater sacrifices than industry, this country is going to have its greatest shortage of all—a shortage of consumers.

Betty Furness

The instability of the economy is equaled only by the instability of economists.

John H. Williams

Education

This will never be a civilized country until we expend more money for books than we do for chewing gum.

Elbert Hubbard

Enlighten the people generally, and tyranny and oppressions of both body and mind will vanish like evil spirits at the dawn of day.

Thomas Jefferson

Ignorance is an evil weed, which dictators may cultivate among their dupes, but which no democracy can afford among its citizens.

William Beveridge

Knowledge itself is power.

Francis Bacon

The foundation of every state is the education of its youth.

Diogenes

On the diffusion of education among the people rest the preservation and perpetuation of our free institutions.

Daniel Webster

I oppose federal aid to education because no one has been able to prove the need for it.

Ronald Reagan

Education is a weapon, whose effects depend on who holds it in his hands and at whom it is aimed.

Joseph Stalin

Next in importance to freedom and justice is popular education, without which neither freedom nor justice can be permanently maintained.

James A. Garfield

Academic freedom can get you killed.

Spiro T. Agnew

The tax which will be paid for the purpose of education is not more than one-thousandth part of what will be paid to kings, priests and nobles who will rise up among us if we leave the people in ignorance.

Thomas Jefferson

Only the educated are free.

Epictetus

Education makes a people easy to lead, but difficult to drive; easy to govern but impossible to enslave.

Henry Peter

What is the first part of politics? Education. The second? Education. And the third? Education.

Jules Michelet

Anti-intellectualism has long been the anti-Semitism of the businessman.

Adlai Stevenson

Whenever the cause of the people is entrusted to professors it is lost.

Nikolai Lenin

In large states public education will always be mediocre, for the same reason that in large kitchens the cooking is usually bad.

Friedrich Nietzsche

To scholars who become politicians the comic role is usually assigned: they have to be the good conscience of a state policy.

Friedrich Nietzsche

Education is the cheap defense of nations.

Edmund Burke

Education . . . has produced a vast population able to read but unable to distinguish what is worth reading.

George Trevelyan

If we value the pursuit of knowledge we must be free to follow wherever that search may lead us.

Adlai Stevenson

The greatest innovation in the world is the demand for education as a right of man; it is a disguised demand for comfort.

Jakob Burckhardt

Political history is far too criminal a subject to be a fit thing to teach children.

W. H. Auden

To America one schoolmaster is worth a dozen poets, and the invention of a machine or the improvement of an implement is of more importance than a masterpiece of Raphael.

Benjamin Franklin

What does education often do? It makes a straight-cut ditch of a free, meandering brook.

Henry David Thoreau

Knowledge is the conformity of the object and the intellect.

Averröes

Upon the education of the people of this country the fate of this country depends.

Benjamin Disraeli

It might be said that I have the best of both worlds: a Harvard education and a Yale degree.

John F. Kennedy

Schools need not preach political doctrine to defend democracy. If they shape men capable of critical thought and trained in social attitudes, that is all that is necessary.

Albert Einstein

Elections

American youth attributes much more importance to arriving at driver's-license age than at voting age.

Marshall McLuhan

America is a land where a citizen will cross the ocean to fight for democracy and won't cross the street to vote in a national election.

Bill Vaughan

Politics has got so expensive that it takes a lot of money even to get beat with.

Will Rogers

Politics is the gentle art of getting votes from the poor and campaign funds from the rich, by promising to protect each from the other.

Oscar Ameringer

When one may pay out over two million dollars to presidential and Congressional campaigns, the U.S. government is virtually up for sale.

John Gardner

It shall be unlawful for any national bank, or any corporation organized by authority of any laws of Congress to make a money contribution in connection with election to any political office.

Act of U.S. Congress, 1907

It makes no difference who you vote for—the two parties are really one party representing 4 percent of the people.

Gore Vidal

The death of democracy is not likely to be assassination by ambush. It will be slow extinction from apathy, indifference and undernourishment.

Robert Maynard Hutchins

An elected official is one who gets 51 percent of the vote cast by 40 percent of the 60 percent of voters who registered.

Dan Bennett

The mandate of November's elections must be the vote of the people—not by default of the people.

Lyndon B. Johnson

Have you ever seen a candidate talking to a rich person on television?

Art Buchwald

The idea that you can merchandise candidates for high office like breakfast cereal . . . is the ultimate indignity to the democratic process.

Adlai Stevenson

For the great majority of mankind are satisfied with appearances, as though they were realities, and are often more influenced by the things that seem than by those that are.

Niccolò Machiavelli

A politician should have three hats. One for throwing in the ring, one for talking through, and one for pulling rabbits out of if elected.

Carl Sandburg

A national campaign is better than the best circus ever heard of, with a mass baptism and a couple of hangings thrown in. It is better, even, than war.

H. L. Mencken

Whatever I do will depend on whether or not it will help me get the nomination.

George Bush

Promises don't fill the belly.

C. H. Spurgeon

Public interest is a term used by every politician to support his ideas.

W. M. Kiplinger

I don't know much about Americanism, but it's a damned good word with which to carry an election.

Warren G. Harding

The man who can make others laugh secures more votes for a measure than the man who forces them to think.

Malcolm de Chazal

I'm not smart enough to lie.

Ronald Reagan

The election isn't very far off when a candidate can recognize you across the street.

Kin Hubbard

Political platforms are for one party to stand on, and the other to jump on.

Arnold H. Glasow

Before you can become a statesman you first have to get elected, and to get elected you have to be a politician pledging support for what the voters want.

Margaret Chase Smith

In politics, familiarity doesn't breed contempt. It breeds voters.

Paul Lazarsfeld

It is not a smear, if you please, if you point out the record of your opponent.

Murray Chotiner

Race prejudice, class prejudice, religious prejudice, are three great forces to which the politician may appeal successfully.

J. H. Wallis

There is a certain satisfaction in coming down to the lowest ground of politics, for we get rid of cant and hypocrisy.

Ralph Waldo Emerson

He who slings mud generally loses ground.

Adlai Stevenson

A candidate running for Congress hired two assistants: one to dig up the facts and the other to bury them.

Anonymous

The saddest life is that of a political aspirant under democracy. His failure is ignominious and his success is disgraceful.

H. L. Mencken

They [candidates] are chosen normally for quite different reasons, the chief of which is simply their power to impress and enchant the intellectually underprivileged.

H. L. Mencken

The first thing you do when you want to get elected is to prostitute yourself. You show me a man with courage and conviction and I'll show you a loser.

Ray Kroc

I do not choose to run.

Calvin Coolidge

If nominated I will not run; if elected, I will not serve.

William T. Sherman

I am now seasoned enough to have learned that the hardest thing about any political campaign is how to win without proving that you are unworthy of winning.

Adlai Stevenson

Plebiscite, n. A popular vote to ascertain the will of the sovereign.

Ambrose Bierce

We must as second best . . . take the least of the evils.

Aristotle

Vote for the man who promises least; he'll be the least disappointing.

Bernard Baruch

Vote early and vote often.

American saying, 1858

Whenever a fellow tells me he's bipartisan, I know he's going to vote against me.

Harry S Truman

Politics is not the art of the possible. It consists in choosing between the disastrous and the unpalatable.

John Kenneth Galbraith

The citizen does not so much vote for a candidate as make a psychological purchase of him.

Joe McGinnis

The right of the citizens of the United States to vote shall not be denied or abridged by the United States or by any state on account of sex.

Nineteenth Amendment, U.S. Constitution, 1920

Do you ever get the feeling that the only reason we have elections is to find out if the polls were right?

Robert Orben

More men have been elected between Sundown and Sunup than ever were elected between Sunup and Sundown.

Will Rogers

People only leave by way of the box—ballot or coffin.

Claiborne Pell

Voters quickly forget what a man says.

Richard M. Nixon

The short memories of American voters is what keeps our politicians in office.

Will Rogers

The man who can right himself by a vote will seldom resort to a musket.

James Fenimore Cooper

Where annual elections end, there slavery begins.

John Adams

In politics women . . . type the letters, lick the stamps, distribute the pamphlets and get out the vote. Men get elected.

Clare Boothe Luce

This struggle and scramble for office, for a way to live without work, will finally test the strength of our institutions.

Abraham Lincoln

In a change of government, the poor seldom change anything except the name of their master.

Phaedrus

Environment

Growing and decaying vegetation in this land are responsible for 93 percent of the oxides of nitrogen.

Ronald Reagan

Put the president of the Sierra Club in a sealed garage with a tree. Put Ronald Reagan in a sealed garage with a running automobile. Wait to see which one of them yells to get out first.

***San Jose Mercury News* editorial**

The need for development of natural resources does not justify writing off the environment.

Felix G. Rohatyn

The first law of ecology is that everything is related to everything else.

Barry Commoner

Hurt not the earth, neither the sea, nor the trees.

Revelation 7:3

America's lands may be ravaged as a result of the actions of the environmentalists.

James Watt

Western civilization is a man running with increased speed through an air-sealed tunnel in search of additional oxygen.

Philip Slater

Man is a complex being: he makes deserts bloom—and lakes die.

Gil Stern

Obviously, the answer to oil spills is to paper-train the tankers.

Ralph Nader

Man masters nature not by force but by understanding.

Jacob Bronowski

There are no passengers on Spaceship Earth. Everybody's crew.

Marshall McLuhan

No witchcraft, no enemy action had silenced the rebirth of new life. . . . The people have done it themselves.

Rachel Carson

If you've seen one redwood, you've seen them all.

Ronald Reagan

European countries . . . treat timber as a crop. We treat timber resources as if they were a mine.

Franklin D. Roosevelt

Any fool can destroy trees. They cannot run away; and if they could, they would still be destroyed—chased and hunted down as long as fun or a dollar could be got out of their dark hides.

John Muir

I have found that the brown bears are under the jurisdiction of the Secretary of Agriculture, the grizzly bears under the care of the Secretary of Interior, and the polar bears under my protection as Secretary of Commerce.

Herbert Hoover

The greatest domestic problem facing our country is saving our soil and water. Our soil belongs also to unborn generations.

Sam Rayburn

The "control of nature" is a phrase conceived in arrogance, born of the Neanderthal age of biology and the convenience of man.

Rachel Carson

When a man wants to murder a tiger he calls it sport; when the tiger wants to murder him he calls it ferocity.

George Bernard Shaw

Children alive today may live to see the first man on Mars and the last elm tree in the United States.

Buffalo News

Man shapes himself through the decisions that shape his environment.

René Dubos

Pollution is nothing but resources we're not harvesting.

Buckminster Fuller

About 14,000 lives were saved in 1978 as a result of improvements in air quality since 1970.

President's Council on Environmental Quality, 1980

We have probed the earth, excavated it, burned it, ripped things from it, buried things in it. . . . That does not fit my definition of a good tenant. If we were here on a month-to-month basis, we would have been evicted long ago.

Rose Elizabeth Bird

As cruel a weapon as the cave man's club, the chemical barrage has been hurled against the fabric of life.

Rachel Carson

Thank God, men cannot as yet fly, and lay waste the sky as well as the earth! We are safe on that side for the present.

Henry David Thoreau

Man is demolishing nature. . . . We are killing things that keep us alive.

Thor Heyerdahl

The only means of conservation is innovation.

Peter Drucker

We are locked into a system of "fouling our own nest" so long as we behave only as independent, rational free-enterprisers.

Garret Hardin

Sanctions against polluters are feeble and out of date, and, in any case, are rarely invoked.

Ralph Nader

The most alarming of all man's assaults upon the environment is the contamination of air, earth, rivers and sea. . . . This pollution is for the most part irrecoverable.

Rachel Carson

In wilderness is the preservation of the world.

Henry David Thoreau

Such prosperity as we have known it up to the present is the consequence of rapidly spending the planet's irreplaceable capital.

Aldous Huxley

It becomes increasingly obvious to all countries that the uneven distribution and consumption of resources . . . is morally, ethically and practically unacceptable.

Moshe Safdie

Many people live in ugly wastelands, but in the absence of imaginative standards, most of them do not even know it.

C. Wright Mills

We abuse land because we regard it as a commodity belonging to us. When we see land as a community to which we belong, we may begin to use it with love and respect.

Aldo Leopold

The day, water, sun, moon, night—I do not have to purchase these things with money.

Plautus

Water and politics don't mix.

William Mulholland

We will use the budget system to be the excuse to make major [environmental] policy decisions.

James Watt

We have not inherited the earth from our fathers; we are borrowing it from our children.

Lester Brown

(In)Equality

All animals are equal, but some animals are more equal than others.

George Orwell

It is the mark of the cultured man that he is aware of the fact that equality is an ethical and not a biological principle.

Ashley Montagu

There is an inequality of right and authority which emanates from God himself.

Pope Leo XIII

That's part of American greatness, is discrimination. Yes, sir. Inequality, I think, breeds freedom and gives a man opportunity.

Lester Maddox

Wherever there is great property, there is great inequality. . . . For one very rich man, there must be at least five hundred poor.

Adam Smith

We hold these truths to be self-evident—that all men are created equal; that they are endowed by their Creator with certain inalienable rights; that among these are life, liberty and the pursuit of happiness.

Thomas Jefferson

The only stable state is the one in which all men are equal before the law.

Aristotle

Equality is the chief groundwork of equity.

M. E. Montaigne

Men are made by nature unequal. It is vain, therefore, to treat them as if they were equal.

James Anthony Froude

Our new government's foundations are laid, its cornerstone rests, upon the great truth that the Negro is not equal to the white man, that slavery—subordination to the superior race—is his natural and normal condition.

Alexander H. Stephens

Let us be very clear on this matter: if we condemn people to inequality in our society we also condemn them to inequality in our economy.

Lyndon B. Johnson

The equality we want is the most tolerable degree of inequality.

G. C. Lichtenberg

Despite legendary examples of spectacular social mobility, the unequal outcomes of one generation are generally the unequal opportunities of the next.

James Tobin

The defect of equality is that we only desire it with our superiors.

Henry Becque

By law of nature all men are equal.

Domitius Ulpian

The question who is the better man has no place in the condition of mere nature, where . . . all men are equal. The inequality that now is has been introduced by the laws civil.

Thomas Hobbes

The passion for equality produces uniformity which produces mediocrity.

Alexis de Tocqueville

Americans are so enamored of equality that they would rather be equal in slavery than unequal in freedom.

Alexis de Tocqueville

Fanaticism

A fanatic is one who can't change his mind and won't change the subject.

Winston Churchill

The worst vice of the fanatic is his sincerity.

Oscar Wilde

A fanatic is a man that does what he thinks the Lord would do if he knew the facts of the case.

Finley Peter Dunne

Fanaticism is always the child of persecution.

Napoleon Bonaparte

Fanaticism consists in redoubling your effort when you have forgotten your aim.

George Santayana

The tendency to claim God as an ally for our partisan values and ends is . . . the source of all religious fanaticism.

Reinhold Niebuhr

Without fanaticism, one cannot accomplish anything.

Evita Peron

I'd feel complimented if you called me a fanatic. The only ones who make things change are fanatics. If you're not fanatic around here, you can't cut it.

Cesar Chavez

From fanaticism to barbarism is only one step.

Denis Diderot

We were what are known as fanatics, people who really want to see a thing carried through—perhaps too quickly.

Annie Kenney

Fascism

Reactionary concepts plus revolutionary emotion result in Fascist mentality.

Wilhelm Reich

Fascism, which was not afraid to call itself reactionary . . . does not hesitate to call itself illiberal and anti-liberal.

Benito Mussolini

Fascism is Capitalism in decay.

Nikolai Lenin

Because Fascism is a lie, it is condemned to literary sterility. And when it is past, it will have no history, except the bloody history of murder.

Ernest Hemingway

If Fascism came to America, it would be on a program of Americanism.

Huey P. Long

The next step [in a Fascist movement] is to fascinate fools and muzzle the intelligent, by emotional excitement on one hand and terrorism on the other.

Bertrand Russell

Fascism is nothing but capitalist reaction; from the point of view of the proletariat the difference between the types of reaction is meaningless.

Leon Trotsky

Fascism is Capitalism plus Murder.

Upton Sinclair

Fascism, before being a party, is a religion.

Benito Mussolini

The Negro is a born anti-fascist.

Adam Clayton Powell, Jr.

Feminism

Men, their rights and nothing more; woman, their rights and nothing less.

Susan B. Anthony

It certainly must have been a relief for the women of the country to realize that one could be a woman and a lady and yet be thoroughly political.

Pearl S. Buck

I have sacrificed everything in my life that I consider precious in order to advance the political career of my husband.

Pat Nixon

"No matter what your fight," I said, "don't be ladylike! God Almighty made woman and the Rockefeller gang of thieves made the ladies."

Mother Jones

Well, it's hard for a mere man to believe that woman doesn't already have equal rights.

Dwight D. Eisenhower

Human beings are not animals, and I do not want to see sex and sexual differences treated as casually and amorally as dogs and other beasts treat them. I believe this could happen under the ERA.

Ronald Reagan

Resolved, that the women of this nation in 1876, have greater cause for discontent, rebellion and revolution than the men of 1776.

Susan B. Anthony

There is no hope even that woman, with her right to vote, will ever purify politics.

Emma Goldman

Equal rights for the sexes will be achieved when mediocre women occupy high positions.

Françoise Giroud

I consider that women who are authors, lawyers and politicians are monsters.

Pierre Auguste Renoir

A woman reading *Playboy* feels a little like a Jew reading a Nazi manual.

Gloria Steinem

I'm the most liberated woman in the world. Any woman can be liberated if she wants to. First, she has to convince her husband.

Martha Mitchell

If particular care and attention is not paid to the ladies, we are determined to foment a rebellion and will not hold ourselves bound by any laws in which we have no voice or representation.

Abigail Adams

But if God had wanted us to think with our wombs, why did He give us a brain?

Clare Boothe Luce

A woman is but an animal, and an animal not of the highest order.

Edmund Burke

To be successful, a woman has to be much better at her job than a man.

Golda Meir

A woman has to be twice as good as a man to go half as far.

Fannie Hurst

Women are not altogether in the wrong when they refuse the rules of life prescribed to the World, for men only have established them and without their consent.

M. E. Montaigne

There are really not many jobs that actually require a penis or vagina, and all other occupations should be open to everyone.

Gloria Steinem

Of my two "handicaps," being female put many more obstacles in my path than being black.

Shirley Chisholm

Who knows what women can be when they are finally free to become themselves.

Betty Friedan

Man's superiority will be shown, not in the fact that he has enslaved his wife, but that he has made her free.

Eugene V. Debs

Aren't women prudes if they don't and prostitutes if they do?

Kate Millet

I became a feminist as an alternative to becoming a masochist.

Sally Kempton

Rape entered the law through the back door . . . as a property crime of man against man. Woman, of course, was viewed as the property.

Susan Brownmiller

The woman who has been given sexual freedom without real financial and social independence will find herself still bartering.

Gloria Steinem

Once made equal to man, woman becomes his superior.

Socrates

Verily the best of women are those who are content with little.

Mohammed

God made man, and then said I can do better than that and made woman.

Adela Rogers St. Johns

Men are never so tired and harassed as when they have to deal with a woman who wants a raise.

Michael Korda

Women—the greatest undeveloped natural resource in the world today.

Edward Steichen

Flag

If you want a symbolic gesture, don't burn the flag, wash it.
Norman Thomas

A person gets from a symbol the meaning he puts into it.
U.S. Supreme Court

Patriotic societies seem to think that the way to educate school children in a democracy is to stage bigger and better flag-saluting.
S. I. Hayakawa

A star for every State, and a State for every star.
Robert Winthrop

White is for purity, red for valor, blue for justice.
Charles Sumner

Freedom

Necessity is the plea for every infringement of human freedom. It is the argument of tyrants; it is the creed of slaves.

William Pitt, the Younger

Those who expect to reap the blessings of freedom must, like men, undergo the fatigue of supporting it.

Thomas Paine

Those who suppress freedom always do so in the name of law and order.

John Lindsay

Freedom comes from human beings, rather than laws and institutions.

Clarence Darrow

When people are free to do as they please, they usually imitate each other.

Eric Hoffer

There's something contagious about demanding freedom.

Robin Morgan

None can love freedom heartily but good men; the rest love not freedom, but license.

John Milton

The realm of freedom does not commence until the point is passed where labor under compulsory of necessity and of external utility is required.

Karl Marx

Those who deny freedom to others deserve it not for themselves.
Abraham Lincoln

The purpose of freedom is to create it for others.
Bernard Malamud

Freedom, especially a woman's freedom, is a conquest to be made, not a gift to be received. It isn't granted. It must be taken.
Federico Fellini

One should never put on one's best trousers to go out to battle for freedom and truth
Henrik Ibsen

Those who profess to favor freedom, and yet deprecate agitation, are men who want rain without thunder and lightning.
Frederick Douglass

Freedom is that faculty which enlarges the usefulness of all other faculties.
Immanuel Kant

Freedom is the intense claim to obey no one but reason.
Heinrich Mann

Freedom is when bondage is understood.
J. Krishnamurti

The basic test of freedom is perhaps less in what we are free to do than in what we are free not to do.
Eric Hoffer

The history of the world is none other than the progress of the consciousness of freedom.
George Hegel

Freedom is as little lost in a day as won in a day.
Jean Paul Richter

A free society is one where it is safe to be unpopular.
Adlai Stevenson

If I want to be free from any other man's dictation, I must understand that I can have no other man under my control.
W. G. Sumner

You are free and that is why you are lost.

Franz Kafka

We cannot defend freedom abroad by deserting it at home.

Edward R. Murrow

Freedom is nothing else but a chance to be better.

Albert Camus

While the state exists, there is no freedom. When there is freedom, there will be no state.

Nikolai Lenin

The freedom we should seek is not the right to oppress others, but the right to live as we choose and think as we choose where our doing so does not prevent others from doing likewise.

Bertrand Russell

Free at last, free at last. Thank God Almighty, I'm free at last.

Martin Luther King, Jr.

Free Enterprise

After I asked him what he meant, he replied that freedom consisted of the unimpeded right to get rich, to use his ability, no matter what the cost to others, to win advancement.

Norman Thomas

I don't meet competition, I crush it.

Charles Revson

The suppression of civil liberties is to many less a matter for horror than the curtailment of the freedom to profit.

Marya Mannes

Laissez-faire, laissez passer. [No interference, and complete freedom of movement.]

François Quesnay

The American style of individualism.

Herbert Hoover

Yet it is that very individualism, so rampant in the United States, which has also led to the spoliation of the environment and has been at the roots of the neglect of the social services and other community needs.

Daniel Bell

Free enterprise ended in the United States a good many years ago. Big oil, big steel, big agriculture avoid the open marketplace.

Gore Vidal

Private enterprise is ceasing to be free enterprise.

Franklin D. Roosevelt

Laissez-faire, supply-and-demand,—one begins to be weary of all that. Leave all to egoism, to ravenous greed of money, of pleasure, of applause;—it is the gospel of despair.

Thomas Carlyle

The system has never failed us once. But we have failed the system every time we lose faith in the magic of the marketplace.

Ronald Reagan

Private enterprise . . . makes OK private action which would be considered dishonest in public action.

John F. Kennedy

What is a man profited, if he shall gain the whole world, and lose his own soul?

Matthew 16:26

It is ridiculous to call this an industry. This is not. This is rat eat rat, dog eat dog. I'll kill 'em before they kill me. You're talking about the American way of survival of the fittest.

Ray Kroc

Avarice, the spur of industry.

David Hume

I have never believed in abandoning our economy to the ruthless workings of the marketplace regardless of the human suffering that might be ceased.

Bernard Baruch

We have always known that heedless self-interest was bad morals; we know now that it is bad economics.

Franklin D. Roosevelt

"A bargain," said the son. "Here's the rule for bargains—'Do other men for they would do you.' That's the true business precept. All others are counterfeits."

Charles Dickens

The Americans have little faith. They rely on the power of the dollar.

Ralph Waldo Emerson

It is idle to suppose that corporations will not be brought more and more under public control.

Alfred North Whitehead

Commerce and manufacturers, in short, can seldom flourish in any state in which there is not a certain degree of confidence in the justice of government.

Adam Smith

The greatest meliorator of the world is selfish, huckstering trade.

Ralph Waldo Emerson

If America is not to have free enterprise, then she can have no freedom of any sort whatever.

Woodrow Wilson

No man profiteth but by the loss of others.

M. E. Montaigne

Free Press/Free Speech

Congress shall make no law . . . abridging the freedom of speech or of the press.

First Amendment, U.S. Constitution, 1791

Freedom is the freedom to say that two plus two make four. If that is granted, all else follows.

George Orwell

The price of freedom of religion or of speech or of the press is that we must put up with, and even pay for, a good deal of rubbish.

Robert Jackson

It is by the goodness of God that in our country we have those three unspeakably precious things: freedom of speech, freedom of conscience, and the prudence never to practice either of them.

Mark Twain

Were nothing to pass the press but what were suited to the universal gusto, farewell typography!

Joseph Glanvill

To reign by opinion, begin by trampling it under your feet.

Jean Jacques Rousseau

The fundamental argument for freedom of opinion is the doubtfulness of all our beliefs.

Bertrand Russell

What this country needs is more free speech worth listening to.

Hansell B. Duckett

You hear about constitutional rights, free speech and the free press. Every time I hear these words I say to myself, "That man is Red!" . . . You never hear a *real* American talk like that.

Frank Hague

I disapprove of what you say, but I will defend to the death your right to say it.

C. S. Tallentyre

Literature should not be suppressed merely because it offends the moral code of the censor.

William O. Douglas

Our liberty depends on freedom of the press, and that cannot be limited without being lost.

Thomas Jefferson

The only real security for social well-being is the free exercise of men's minds.

Harold J. Laski

Freedom of opinion can only exist when the government thinks itself secure.

Bertrand Russell

Thus I have maintained by English history, that in proportion as the Press has been free, English Government has been secure.

Thomas Erskine

The best test of truth is the power of the thought to get itself accepted in the competition of the market. . . . We should be eternally vigilant against attempts to check the expression that we loathe.

Oliver Wendell Holmes, Jr.

Freedom of the press is the staff of life for any vital democracy.

Wendell Phillips

The key to security is public information.

Margaret Chase Smith

Absolute freedom of the press to discuss public questions is a foundation stone of American liberty.

Herbert Hoover

Where the press is under strict and efficient control, literacy can become a weapon for the support of a universal tyrant.

George S. Counts

It is well to remember that freedom through the press is the thing that comes first. Most of us probably feel we couldn't be free without newspapers, and that is the real reason we want the newspapers to be free.

Edward R. Murrow

Geography

American democracy is fundamentally the outcome of the experiences of the American people in dealing with the West.

Frederick Jackson Turner

What makes a nation in the beginning is a good piece of geography.

Robert Frost

Size is not grandeur, and territory does not make a nation.

Thomas Huxley

In the United States, there is more space where nobody is than where anybody is. This is what makes America what it is.

Gertrude Stein

All that we are proud of in the American character, . . . we may trace to the fact that land has been cheap in the United States, because new soil has been open to the emigrant.

Henry George

If the free land did it all, then we are busted when the free land goes.

Charles A. Beard

There is no safety valve in the form of a Western prairie to which those thrown out of work by the Eastern economic machines can go for a new start.

Franklin D. Roosevelt

Government

I would not give half a guinea to live under one form of government rather than another.

Samuel Johnson

I don't make jokes—I just watch government and report the facts.

Will Rogers

Government is too big and important to be left to the politicians.

Chester Bowles

The basis of our political systems is the right of the people to make and to alter their constitutions of government.

George Washington

Government is itself an art, one of the subtlest of the arts. It is the art of making men live together in peace with reasonable happiness.

Felix Frankfurter

Government, even in its best state, is but a necessary evil; in its worst state, an intolerable one.

Thomas Paine

My brother Bob doesn't want to be in government—he promised Dad he'd go straight.

John F. Kennedy

For in reason, all government without the consent of the governed is the very definition of slavery.

Jonathan Swift

Big Brother is watching you.

George Orwell

All free governments are managed by the combined wisdom and folly of the people.

James A. Garfield

Nothing appears more surprising to those who consider human affairs with a philosophical eye than the easiness with which the many are governed by the few.

David Hume

Today the nations of the world may be divided into two classes— the nations in which government fears the people, and the nations in which the people fear the government.

Amos R. E. Pinchot

The great problem in government is that it never goes bankrupt.

Jerry Brown

Society is produced by our wants, and government by our wickedness.

William Godwin

Accountancy—that is government.

Louis D. Brandeis

The art of government is the organization of idolatry.

George Bernard Shaw

Government is emphatically a machine: to the discontented a "taxing machine," to the contented a "machine for securing property."

Thomas Carlyle

If angels were to govern men, neither external nor internal controls on government would be necessary

James Madison

Government is only as good as the men in it.

Drew Pearson

That form of government is the best that includes monarchy, aristocracy, and democracy.

Polybius

Each generation . . . has a right to choose for itself the form of government it believes most promotive of its own happiness.

Thomas Jefferson

. . . . A government of laws, and not of men.

John Adams

The art of government consists in taking as much money as possible from one class of citizens to give to the other.

Voltaire

Government is an association of men who do violence to the rest of us.

Tolstoi

The first rule in a handbook of government is idleness.

Alain

I fear Washington and centralized government more than I do Moscow.

Barry Goldwater

The office of government is not to confer happiness, but to give men opportunity to work out happiness for themselves.

William Ellery Channing

All religions, laws, moral and political systems are but necessary means to preserve social order.

Ch'en Tu-hsiu

All well-governed states and wise princes have taken care not to reduce the nobility to despair, nor the people to discontent.

Niccolò Machiavelli

To govern means to rectify.

Confucius

Government has been a fossil; it should be a plant.

Ralph Waldo Emerson

Whenever any Form of Government becomes destructive . . . it is the Right of the People to alter or abolish it.

Declaration of Independence

Government after all is a very simple thing.

Warren G. Harding

Health

The health of the people is really the foundation upon which all their happiness and all their powers as a state depend.

Benjamin Disraeli

A physician and a priest ought not to belong to any particular nation and should be divested of all political opinions.

Napoleon Bonaparte

Many dishes, many diseases. Many medicines, few cures.

Benjamin Franklin

Thousands upon thousands of persons have studied disease. Almost no one has studied health.

Adelle Davis

It is the sick who need medicine and not the well.

Thomas Jefferson

There's another advantage to being poor—a doctor will cure you faster.

Kin Hubbard

An inescapable lesson of contemporary medicine is that when treatment of a given disease is ineffective or where costs are insupportable, attention must be given to prevention.

Howard R. Hiatt

There is more danger from the doctor than from the disease.

Latin saying

God heals and the doctor takes the fee.

Benjamin Franklin

There are some remedies worse than the disease.

Publilius Syrus

I often say a great doctor kills more people than a great general.

Wilhelm von Leibnitz

Care more for the individual patient than for the special features of the disease.

William Osler

There are more doctors in a single North Shore medical building than in one entire West Side ghetto.

Jack Starr

A hospital bed is a parked taxi with the meter running.

Groucho Marx

Financial ruin from medical bills is almost exclusively an American disease.

Roul Turley

Housing

What is the use of a house if you haven't got a tolerable planet to put it on?

Henry David Thoreau

There's no law saying the Negro has to live in Harlem or Watts.

Ronald Reagan

If you've seen one city slum, you've seen them all.

Spiro T. Agnew

The slum is the measure of civilization.

Jacob Riis

Nobody shoulders a rifle in defense of a boardinghouse.

Bret Harte

To the moderately poor the home is the only place of liberty.

G. K. Chesterton

I see one-third of a nation ill-housed, ill-clad, ill-nourished.

Franklin D. Roosevelt

Immigration

My folks didn't come over on the Mayflower, but they were there to meet the boat.

Will Rogers

America is so rich and fat, because it has eaten the tragedy of millions of immigrants.

Michael Gold

America is God's crucible, the great melting pot where all the races of Europe are melting and re-forming.

Israel Zangwill

Here the melting pot stands open—if you're willing to get bleached first.

Buffy Sainte-Marie

I hear that melting pot stuff a lot, and all I can say is that we haven't melted.

Jesse Jackson

The United States is the only great and populous nation-state and world power whose people are not cemented by ties of blood, race or original language.

Dorothy Thompson

Everyone's quick to blame the alien.

Aeschylus

We heartily approve all legitimate efforts to prevent the United

States from being used as the dumping ground for known criminals and professional paupers of Europe.

Democratic Party platform, 1892

The great social adventure of America is no longer the conquest of the wilderness but the absorption of fifty different peoples.

Walter Lippmann

Give me your tired, your poor,
Your huddled masses yearning to breathe free,
The wretched refuse of your teeming shore,
Send these, the homeless, tempest-tossed, to me:
I lift my lamp beside the golden door.

Emma Lazarus

Not merely a nation but a nation of nations.

Lyndon B. Johnson

America! half brother of the world!
With something good and bad of every land.

P. J. Bailey

Some Americans need hyphens in their names because only part of them has come over.

Woodrow Wilson

There can be no fifty-fifty Americanism in this country. There is room here for only 100 percent Americanism, only for those who are Americans and nothing else.

Theodore Roosevelt

The mission of the United States is one of benevolent assimilation.
William McKinley

Remember always that all of us, and you and I especially, are descended from immigrants and revolutionists.

Franklin D. Roosevelt

E pluribus unum. [From many, one.]

U.S. motto

Foreign immigration, which in the past has added so much to the wealth, development of resources, and increase of power to the nation . . . should be fostered and encouraged by a liberal and just policy.

Republican Party platform, 1864

Out of twelve families of immigrants of each country, generally seven Scotch will succeed, nine German, and four Irish.

J. Hector St. John

'Tis not likely that any man of a plentiful estate should voluntarily abandon a happy certainty to roam after imaginary advantages in a new world.

Robert Beverley

It would be a sight hitherto unknown on earth if men forsook their home without being either pushed or pulled.

Thomas B. Reed

Canada has never been a melting pot; more like a tossed salad.

Arnold Edinborough

Imperialism

At the moment the United States is the most powerful, the most prosperous and the most dangerous country in the world.

Robert Maynard Hutchins

An inevitable link in a chain of logical sequences: industry, markets, control, navy bases.

Alfred Thayer Mahan

Imperialism is the transition stage from capitalism to socialism. . . . It is capitalism dying, not dead.

Nikolai Lenin

There should be no mystery about American purposes abroad. We want a world hospitable to our society and to our ideals.

Alexander Haig

I think we must save America from the missionary idea that you must get the whole world on to the American way of life. This is really a big world danger.

John Gunther

Americans think of themselves as a huge rescue squad on twenty-four-hour call to any spot on the globe where dispute and conflict may erupt.

Eldridge Cleaver

I took the Canal Zone and let Congress debate, and while the debate goes on the canal does too.

Theodore Roosevelt

For our democracy has been marred by imperialism, and it has been enlightened only by individual and sporadic efforts at freedom.

Pearl S. Buck

It is our manifest destiny to lead and rule all nations.

James Gordon Bennett

No man has a right to fix the boundary of the march of a nation; no man has a right to say to his country—thus far shalt thou go and no further.

Theodore Parker

I don't feel we did wrong in taking this great country away from them. There were great numbers of people who needed new land, and the Indians were selfishly trying to keep it for themselves.

John Wayne

No colonization without misrepresentation.

Simeon Strunsky

I am going to teach the South American republics to elect good men.

Woodrow Wilson

We should keep [the Panama Canal]. After all, we stole it fair and square.

S. I. Hayakawa

I confess that I cannot understand how we can plot, lie, cheat and commit murder abroad and remain humane, honorable, trustworthy and trusted at home.

Archibald Cox

Poor Mexico, so far from God and so close to the United States.

Porfirio Díaz

The world must be made safe for democracy.

Woodrow Wilson

The American continents . . . are henceforth not to be considered as subjects for future colonization by any European powers.

James Monroe

All colonies are oppressed people.

Nikolai Lenin

In the eyes of empire builders men are not men, but instruments.

Napoleon Bonaparte

The day of small nations has long passed away. The day of Empires has come.

Joseph Chamberlain

We don't know what we want, but we are ready to bite somebody to get it.

Will Rogers

Inflation

Inflation is the one form of taxation that can be imposed without legislation.

Milton Friedman

The best way to destroy the capitalist system is to debauch the currency. By a continuing process of inflation, governments can confiscate, secretly and unobserved, an important part of the wealth of their citizens.

Nikolai Lenin

The first panacea for a mismanaged nation is inflation of the currency; the second is war. Both bring a temporary prosperity; both bring a permanent ruin.

Ernest Hemingway

Inflation is bringing us true democracy. For the first time in history, luxuries and necessities are selling at the same price.

Robert Orben

There is no direct or indirect connection between deficits and inflation.

William Niskanen

Inflation is repudiation.

Calvin Coolidge

Integration

Segregation Now, Segregation Tomorrow, Segregation Forever.
George Wallace

We conclude that in the field of public education, the doctrine of "separate but equal" has no place. Separate educational facilities are inherently unequal.
U.S. Supreme Court, 1954

They put Negroes in the schools, and now they've driven God out.
George Wallace

The Bible speaks about racial segregation, so we don't let students date interracially. That's not discrimination. That's religion.
Bob Jones, Jr.

Segregation is the offspring of an illicit intercourse between injustice and immorality.
Martin Luther King, Jr.

A radically integrated community is a chronological term timed from the entrance of the first black family to the exit of the last white family.
Saul Alinsky

Forced integration is just as wrong as forced segregation.
Barry Goldwater

What we mean by integration is not to be with them [whites] but to have what they have.
Julian Bond

To like an individual because he's black is just as insulting as to dislike him because he isn't white.

e. e. cummings

Integration today means the man who "makes it" leaving his black brothers behind in the ghetto as fast as his new sports car will take him.

Stokely Carmichael

Negro, n. The *pièce de résistance* in the American political problem. Representing him by the letter n, the Republicans begin to build their equation thus: "Let n = the white man." This, however, appears to give an unsatisfactory solution.

Ambrose Bierce

In all things that are purely social we can be as separate as the fingers yet one as the hand in all things essential to mutual progress.

Booker T. Washington

Internationalism

There can be no law if we were to invoke one code of international conduct for those who oppose us and another for our friends.

Dwight D. Eisenhower

In Paris they simply stared when I spoke to them in French; I never did succeed in making those idiots understand their own language.

Mark Twain

The United States has the power to destroy the world, but not the power to save it alone.

Margaret Mead

Foreign Aid—taxing poor people in rich countries for the benefit of rich people in poor countries.

Bernard Rosenberg

The health of nations is more important than the wealth of nations.

Will Durant

We prefer world law, in the age of self-determination, to world war in the age of mass extermination.

John F. Kennedy

This organization [United Nations] is created to prevent you from going to hell. It isn't created to take you to heaven.

Henry Cabot Lodge II

The League of Nations is a declaration of love without the promise of marriage.

Alfred von Tirpitz

Traditional nationalism cannot survive the fissioning of the atom. One world or none.

Stuart Chase

My country is the world. My countrymen are all mankind.

William Lloyd Garrison

I am not an Athenian or a Greek, but a citizen of the world.

Socrates

A man's feet should be planted in his country, but his eyes should survey the world.

George Santayana

Genius is of no country.

Charles Churchill

We are citizens of the world; and the tragedy of our times is that we do not know this.

Woodrow Wilson

The man who loves other countries as much as his own stands on a level with the man who loves other women as much as he loves his own wife.

Theodore Roosevelt

No government can remain stable in an unstable society and an unstable world.

Léon Blum

The journey of a thousand leagues begins with a single step. So we must never neglect any work of peace within our reach, however small.

Adlai Stevenson

Human sovereignty transcends national sovereignty.

Lester B. Pearson

Isolationism

Peace, commerce and honest friendship with all nations—entangling alliances with none.

Thomas Jefferson

Every time Europe looks across the Atlantic to see the American eagle, it observes only the rear end of an ostrich.

H. G. Wells

The less America looks abroad, the grander its promise.

Ralph Waldo Emerson

If you wish to avoid foreign collision, you had better abandon the ocean.

Henry Clay

Justice

There is no such thing as justice—in or out of court.

Clarence Darrow

Punishment is an artificial consequence annexed by political authority to an offensive act.

Jeremy Bentham

This is a court of law, young man, not a court of justice.

Oliver Wendell Holmes, Jr.

Justice, n. A commodity which in a more or less adulterated condition the State sells to the citizen as a reward for his allegiance, taxes and personal service.

Ambrose Bierce

No matter whether th' constitution follows th' flag or not, th' supreme coort follows th' iliction returns.

Finley Peter Dunne

Man's capacity for justice makes democracy possible, but man's inclination to injustice makes democracy necessary.

Reinhold Niebuhr

Justice is incidental to law and order.

J. Edgar Hoover

Injustice is relatively easy to bear; what stings is justice.

H. L. Mencken

Justice is the right of the weaker.

Joseph Joubert

Every human being has a responsibility for injustice anywhere in the community.

Scott Buchanan

Since when do you have to agree with people to defend them from injustice?

Lillian Hellman

Unless justice be done to others it will not be done to us.

Woodrow Wilson

Why should there not be a patient confidence in the ultimate justice of the people?

Abraham Lincoln

Trial, n. A formal inquiry designed to prove and put upon record the blameless characters of judges, advocates and jurors. . . .

Ambrose Bierce

National injustice is the surest road to national downfall.

William Evarts

A kingdom founded on injustice never lasts.

Seneca

Judging from the main portions of the history of the world, so far, justice is always in jeopardy.

Walt Whitman

It was the old notion that justice should not arise from laws, but laws from justice.

Joseph Joubert

The sword of the law should never fall but on those whose guilt is so apparent as to be pronounced by their friends as well as foes.

Thomas Jefferson

Love of justice in the generality of men is only the fear of suffering from injustice.

La Rochefoucauld

Justice is the end of government.

Daniel Defoe

Labor

One cannot walk through a mass-production factory and not feel that one is in hell.

W. H. Auden

Labor is prior to, and independent of, capital. Capital is only the fruit of labor and would never have existed if labor had not existed first.

Abraham Lincoln

Labor unions are the worst thing that ever struck the earth because they take away a man's independence.

Henry Ford

Show me the country in which there are no strikes and I'll show you that country in which there is no liberty.

Emma Goldman

It is essential that there should be organizations of labor. This is an era of organization. Capital organizes and therefore labor must organize.

Theodore Roosevelt

Labor in a white skin cannot be free as long as labor in a black skin is branded.

Karl Marx

The labor union is an elemental response to the human instinct for group action in dealing with group problems.

William Green

There is no real wealth but the labor of man.

Percy Bysshe Shelley

Freedom of contract begins where equality of bargaining power begins.

Oliver Wendell Holmes, Jr.

There is no right to strike against the public safety by anybody, anywhere, anytime.

Calvin Coolidge

Fight labor's demands to the last ditch and there will come a time when it seizes the whole of power, makes itself sovereign and takes what it used to ask for.

Walter Lippmann

Long ago we stated the reason for labor organization. We said that a union was essential to give laborers opportunity to deal on an equality with their employer.

U.S. Supreme Court

The workers are the saviors of society, the redeemers of the race.

Eugene V. Debs

The strike is the weapon of the industrial jungle.

Sidney Hillman

It is labour . . . which puts the greatest part of value upon land, without which it would scarcely be worth anything.

John Locke

Wages are the measure of dignity that society puts on a job.

Johnnie Tillmon

At present, the support of a family is a hidden tax on the wage earner—his wage buys the labor power of two people.

Margaret Benston

Labor, like Israel, has many sorrows.

John L. Lewis

Have you ever told a coal miner in West Virginia or Kentucky that what he needs is individual initiative to go out and get a job where there isn't any?

Robert F. Kennedy

For the wage-earner gets his living on sufferance: while he continues to please his employer he may earn a living.

Suzanne LaFollette

The main impact of the computer has been the provision of unlimited jobs for clerks.

Peter Drucker

The labor of a human being is not a commodity or article of commerce.

Clayton Antitrust Act, 1914

Great parts of our economy are directly dependent upon women having a weak self-concept. . . . A woman who does not know who she is can be sold anything.

Gabrielle Burton

The strike is a phenomenon of war.

Georges Sorel

It is questionable if all the mechanical inventions yet made have lightened the day's toil of any human being.

John Stuart Mill

One half of the world must sweat and groan that the other half may dream.

Henry Wadsworth Longfellow

The prosecution of modern war rests completely upon the operation of labor in mines, mills and factories, so that labor fights there just as truly as the soldiers do in the trenches.

Mary Ritter Beard

Labor is the capital of our workingmen.

Grover Cleveland

He that defraudeth a laborer of his hire is a bloodshedder.

Ecclesiasticus 34

The proletarians have nothing to lose but their chains. They have a world to win. Workers of the world unite!

Karl Marx and Friedrich Engels

Law

Of course there's a different law for the rich and the poor; otherwise, who would go into business?

E. Ralph Stewart

What do I care about the Law? Hain't I got the power?

Cornelius Vanderbilt

Law is merely the expression of the will of the strongest for the time being, and therefore laws have no fixity, but shift from generation to generation.

Charles A. Madison

Law and equity are two things that God hath joined, but which man hath put asunder.

Charles C. Colton

Under current law, it is a crime for a private citizen to lie to a government official, but not for a government official to lie to the people.

Douglas M. Fraser

Nobody has a more sacred obligation to obey the law than those who make the law.

Sophocles

Law and order are always and everywhere the law and order which protect the established hierarchy.

Herbert Marcuse

To make laws that man cannot, and will not obey, serves to bring all law into contempt.

Elizabeth Cady Stanton

The mass of the people have nothing to do with the laws but to obey them.

Samuel Horsley

Good men must not obey the laws too well.

Ralph Waldo Emerson

Laws are like cobwebs, which may catch small flies, but let wasps and hornets break through.

Jonathan Swift

No person shall be . . . deprived of life, liberty, or property, without due process of law.

Fifth Amendment, U.S. Constitution, 1791

Little money, little law.

Anonymous, 1550

Lawyers are the only persons in whom ignorance of the law is not punished.

Jeremy Bentham

A jury consists of twelve persons chosen to decide who has the better lawyer.

Robert Frost

Who will protect the public when the police violate the law?

Ramsey Clark

Of the faults traditionally attributed to democracy one only is fairly chargeable on the United States . . . the disposition to be lax in enforcing laws disliked by any large part of the population.

James Bryce

Where the weak or oppressed assert the rights that have been so long denied them, those in power inevitably resist on the basis of the necessity for tranquillity.

Earl Warren

Extreme law is often extreme injustice.

Terence

When I hear any man talk of an unalterable law, the only effect it produces upon me is to convince me that he is an unalterable fool.

Sydney Smith

Law is a reflection and a source of prejudice. It both enforces and suggests forms of bias.

Diane B. Schulder

Law is order, and good law is good order.

Aristotle

In a democracy only those laws which have their bases in folkways or the approval of strong groups have a chance of being enforced.

Abraham Myerson

The law is a sort of hocus-pocus science.

Charles Macklin

We must observe the moralistic attitude toward law in America, expressed in the common belief that there is a higher law.

Gunnar Myrdal

Law is a pledge that the citizens of a state will do justice to one another.

Lycophron

Law stands mute in the midst of arms.

Cicero

A lawyer with a briefcase can steal more than a hundred men with guns.

Mario Puzo

New lords, new laws.

John Harington

Law is but a heathen word for prayer.

Daniel Defoe

In law, nothing is certain but the expense.

Samuel Butler

Litigious terms, fat contentions, and flowing fees.

John Milton

Laws were made to be broken.

Christopher North

Law is a formless mass of isolated decisions.

Morris Cohen

Laws do not persuade because they threaten.

Seneca

There are not enough jails, not enough policemen, not enough courts to enforce a law not supported by the people.

Hubert Humphrey

Lawful, adj. Compatible with the will of a judge having jurisdiction.

Ambrose Bierce

The welfare of the people is the chief law.

Cicero

The laws of a nation form the most instructive portion of its history.

Edward Gibbon

The United States is the greatest law factory the world has ever known.

Charles Evans Hughes

The law, in its majestic equality, forbids all men to sleep under bridges, to beg in the streets, and to steal bread—the rich as well as the poor.

Anatole France

The violation of some laws is a normal part of the behavior of every citizen.

Stuart Chase

From Antigone through Martin Luther to Martin Luther King the issue of liberty has turned on the existence of a higher law than that of the State.

Milton Mayer

Leadership

Greater love hath no man than this, that he lay down his friends for his political life.

Jeremy Thorpe

Leadership appears to be the art of getting others to want to do something you are convinced should be done.

Vance Packard

It's possible to dazzle a crowd if you really work at it. But that is no qualification for leadership. Hitler was a master of crowds.

George McGovern

If you can't convince them, confuse them.

Harry S Truman

There go my people. I must find out where they are going so I can lead them.

Alexander Ledru-Rollin

I must follow the people. Am I not their leader?

Benjamin Disraeli

Political ability is the ability to foretell what is going to happen tomorrow, next week, next month and next year. And to have the ability afterwards to explain why it didn't happen.

Winston Churchill

Since a politician never believes what he says, he is always astonished when others do.

Charles de Gaulle

The ruler over a country of a thousand chariots must give diligent attention to business; he must be sincere; he must be economical; he must love his people; and he must provide employment for them at the proper seasons.

Confucius

Not to decide is to decide.

Harvey Cox

As for the men in power, they are so anxious to establish the myth of infallibility that they do their utmost to ignore truth.

Boris Pasternak

It is hard to look up to a leader who keeps his ear to the ground.

James H. Boren

In all legislative assemblies, the greater the number composing them may be, the fewer will be the men who will in fact direct their proceedings.

Alexander Hamilton

Leadership is action, not position.

Donald H. McGannon

We're going to move left and right at the same time.

Jerry Brown

Perhaps one of the most important accomplishments of my administration has been minding my own business.

Calvin Coolidge

It is frequently a misfortune to have very brilliant men in charge of affairs; they expect too much of ordinary men.

Thucydides

Reason and judgment are the qualities of a leader.

Tacitus

The final test of a leader is that he leaves behind in other men the conviction and the will to carry on.

Walter Lippmann

Those who govern most make the least noise.

John Sidden

Distrust all men in whom the impulse to punish is powerful.

Friedrich Nietzsche

Nothing doth more hurt in a state than that cunning men pass for wise.

Francis Bacon

Everyone wants my blood, but no one wants my job.

Guy Mollet

There are very few so foolish that they had not rather govern themselves than be governed by others.

Thomas Hobbes

Rulers are men before God and gods before men.

Nathaniel Ames

Thus in the highest position there is the least freedom of action.

Sallust

With how little wisdom the world is governed.

Count Oxenstierna

When the best leader's work is done, the people say, "We did it ourselves."

Lao-tzu

Liberalism

America has had gifted conservative statesmen and national leaders. . . . But with few exceptions, only the liberals have gone down in history as national heroes.

Gunnar Myrdal

I can remember way back when a liberal was one who was generous with his own money.

Will Rogers

The worst enemy of the new radicals are the old liberals.

Nikolai Lenin

A liberal is a man too broadminded to take his own side in a quarrel.

Robert Frost

The radical of one country is the conservative of the next. The radical invents the views. When he has worn them out the conservative adopts them.

Mark Twain

The southern liberal has a certain kind of intensity that's almost impossible to achieve in the North.

Tom Hayden

Liberalism is child's play; revolution is a force.

Otto von Bismarck

What the liberal really wants is to bring about change which will not in any way endanger his position.

Stokely Carmichael

Liberalism . . . is the supreme form of generosity; it is the right which the majority concedes to minorities and hence it is the noblest cry that has ever resounded on this planet.

José Ortega y Gasset

The concept of the self-made man has been the key to America's liberalism.

Garry Wills

The main principle and foundation of liberalism is the rejection of the divine law.

Pope Leo XIII

Liberal institutions straightway cease from being liberal the moment they are soundly established.

Friedrich Nietzsche

I would call the Democratic Left . . . the group which secures social advancement for all the people in a framework of freedom and consent.

Luis Muñoz Marin

Liberty

Proclaim liberty throughout all the land unto all the inhabitants thereof.

Leviticus 25:10

It is a great and dangerous error to suppose that all people are equally entitled to liberty.

John C. Calhoun

Liberty is the one thing you can't have unless you give it to others.
William Allen White

Liberty doesn't work as well in practice as it does in speeches.
Will Rogers

The people never give up their liberties but under some delusion.
Edmund Burke

They that give up essential liberty to obtain a little temporary safety deserve neither liberty nor safety.

Benjamin Franklin

Liberty is always dangerous, but it is the safest thing we have.
Harry Emerson Fosdick

The tree of liberty must be refreshed from time to time with the blood of patriots and tyrants. It is its natural manure.

Thomas Jefferson

Liberty means responsibility. That is why most men dread it.
George Bernard Shaw

Liberty, n. One of Imagination's most precious possessions.

Ambrose Bierce

Few men desire liberty; most men wish only for a just master.

Sallust

The history of liberty is the history of resistance.

Woodrow Wilson

Liberty is so much latitude as the powerful choose to accord to the weak.

Learned Hand

I know not what course others may take, but as for me, give me liberty, or give me death!

Patrick Henry

The price we have to pay for money is paid in liberty.

Robert Louis Stevenson

Wherever public spirit prevails, liberty is secure.

Noah Webster

Mankind is tired of liberty.

Benito Mussolini

Only in states in which the power of the people is supreme has liberty any abode.

Cicero

The contest for ages has been to rescue liberty from the grasp of executive power.

Daniel Webster

Liberty, equality, fraternity.

Motto of the French Republic

Liberties and masters are not easily combined.

Tacitus

By fraternity only will liberty be saved.

Victor Hugo

Modern liberty begins in revolt.

H. M. Kallen

Liberty is the sovereignty of the individual.

Josiah Warren

Liberties . . . depend on the silence of the law.

Thomas Hobbes

Liberty is the power that we have over ourselves.

Hugo Grotius

He that would make his own liberty secure must guard even his enemy from oppression.

Thomas Paine

Lobbying

Lobbying is declared to be a crime.

Georgia State Constitution, 1877

Lobbyists are the touts of protected industries.

Winston Churchill

A Lobbyist is a person that is supposed to help a Politician to make up his mind, not only help him but pay him.

Will Rogers

Lobbying is built into the American system. Teachers and labor unions do it. Why shouldn't foreign countries?

Tongsun Park

We came to a decision some time ago that the only way we could change the political fortunes of the petroleum industry was to change Congress.

Harold Scroggins

Majority

The principle of majority rule is the mildest form in which force of number can be exercised. It is a pacific substitute for civil war.

Walter Lippmann

Hain't we got all the fools in town on our side? And ain't that a big enough majority in any town?

Mark Twain

The majority, compose them how you will, are a herd, and not a very nice one.

William Hazlitt

When great changes occur in history, when great principles are involved, as a rule the majority is wrong.

Eugene V. Debs

Decision by majorities is as much an expedient as lighting by gas.

William Ewart Gladstone

If the majority rules, then the earth belongs to colored people.

Charles Victor Roman

Let the people decide.

Stokely Carmichael

Any man more right than his neighbor constitutes a majority of one.

Henry David Thoreau

The test of courage comes when we are in the minority. The test of tolerance comes when we are in the majority.

Ralph W. Sockman

Seven never wait for one.

Russian saying

The voice of the majority is no proof of justice.

J.C.F. von Schiller

One man with courage is a majority.

Thomas Jefferson

A majority is always the best repartee.

Benjamin Disraeli

Whenever you find that you are on the side of the majority, it is time to reform.

Mark Twain

Media

Then hail to the Press! Chosen guardian of freedom! Strong sword-arm of justice! Bright sunbeam of truth!

Horace Greeley

The press is a great industry and therein lies the logic of its behavior.

J.B.S. Hardman

America is the only country in the world where you can go on the air and kid politicians—and where politicians go on the air and kid the people.

Groucho Marx

People everywhere confuse
What they read in newspapers with news.

A. J. Liebling

All I know is what I read in the papers.

Will Rogers

The essential American strategy: publicity.

Richard H. Rovere

Publicity is to a contemporaneous culture what the great public monuments and churches and buildings of state are to more traditional societies, an instrument of solidarity; but because publicity is only generalized gossip of the in-group, the solidarity it creates is synthetic.

Christopher Lasch

The American press today is ninety percent a class monopoly. That means it responds to the pressures and compulsions to which other big business enterprises respond.

Max Lerner

Any man with ambition, integrity—and $10 million—can start a daily newspaper.

Henry Morgan

The bigger the information media, the less courage and freedom they allow. Bigness means weakness.

Eric Sevareid

The message of the medium is the commercial.

Alice Embree

In America the president reigns for four years, and journalism governs for ever and ever.

Oscar Wilde

It is a newspaper's duty to print the news and raise hell.

Chicago Times, **1861**

Journalism consists in buying white paper at two cents a pound and selling it at ten cents a pound.

Charles A. Dana

Newspapers are read at the breakfast and dinner tables. God's great gift to man is appetite. Put nothing in the paper that will destroy it.

W. R. Nelson

Never lose your temper with the press or the public is a major rule of political life.

Christabel Pankhurst

The journalist is partly in the entertainment business and partly in the advertising business.

Claud Cockburn

I am one person who can truthfully say, "I got my job through the *New York Times.*"

John F. Kennedy

A dilemma has to get up pretty early in the morning to fool the *New York Times.*

Edwin Newman

Because systems of mass communication can communicate only officially acceptable levels of reality, no one can know the extent of the secret unconscious life. No one in America can know what will happen. No one is in real control.

Allen Ginsberg

Journalists are interesting. They just aren't as interesting as the things they cover.

Nora Ephron

There are honest journalists like there are honest politicians. When bought, they stay bought.

Bill Moyers

Nobody believes a rumor here in Washington until it's officially denied.

Edward Cheyfitz

Newspaper editors are men who separate the wheat from the chaff, and then print the chaff

Adlai Stevenson

The *New York Times* is the official leak of the State Department.

Mort Sahl

Don't expect news, for I know no more than a newspaper.

Horace Walpole

Were it left to me to decide whether we should have a government without newspapers, or newspapers without a government, I should not hesitate a moment to prefer the latter.

Thomas Jefferson

The difference between literature and journalism is that journalism is unreadable and literature is not read.

Oscar Wilde

A [television] license to print money.

Roy Thomson

A newspaper may somewhat arrogantly assert that it prints "all the news that's fit to print." But no newspaper yet has been moved to declare at the end of each edition, "That's the way it is," as Walter Cronkite does.

Eugene McCarthy

I really look with commiseration over the great body of my fellow citizens who, reading newspapers, live and die in the belief that they have known something of what has been passing in the world in their time.

Harry S Truman

Journalism, like history, is certainly not an exact science.

John Gunther

We live under a government of men and morning newspapers.

Wendell Phillips

The relationship between a reporter and a President is exactly the same as that between a pitcher and a batter . . . they both are trying to keep each other away.

Merriman Smith

Information is the currency of democracy.

Ralph Nader

Television is democracy at its ugliest.

Paddy Chayefsky

This generation, raised on "Eyewitness News," conditioned by the instant replay, and spared the illumination that comes from tedious historical study, tends to be even more ahistorical than most.

Harry S Truman

Democracy makes a government of bullies tempered by editors.

Ralph Waldo Emerson

All the faults of the age come from Christianity and journalism.

Frank Harris

The press is the best instrument for enlightening the mind of man, and improving him as a rational, moral and social being.

Thomas Jefferson

Newspapers always excite curiosity. No one ever lays one down without a feeling of disappointment.

Charles Lamb

The most dreadful thing of all is that millions of people in the poor countries are going to starve to death before our eyes . . . upon our television sets.

C. P. Snow

You [news photographer] furnish the pictures and I'll furnish the war.

William Randolph Hearst

He who is without a newspaper is cut off from his species.

P. T. Barnum

The things that bother a press about a President will ultimately bother the country.

David Halberstam

The government is the only known vessel that leaks from the top.

James Reston

A newspaper is the lowest thing there is!

Richard Daley

Self-government will be more secure if the editorial page recovers the vigor and stature it had before the businessman took over from the editors as top man in journalism.

Herbert Brucker

News is the first rough draft of history.

Benjamin Bradlee

In America journalism is apt to be regarded as an extension of history: in Britian, as an extension of conversation.

Anthony Sampson

Among the calamities of war may be justly numbered the diminuation of the love of truth by the falsehoods which interest dictates and credulity encourages.

Samuel Johnson

Our major obligation is not to mistake slogans for solutions.

Edward R. Murrow

A fourth estate, of able editors, springs up.

Thomas Carlyle

The first essence of journalism is to know what you want to know; the second, is to find out who will tell you.

John Gunther

"The Medium is the Message" because it is the medium that shapes and controls the search and form of human associations and actions.

Marshall McLuhan

World news is becoming local news. Unless we wake up to the fact, we are living in a dreamworld of the past.

Edward Stone

To a newspaperman a human is an item with the skin wrapped around it.

Fred Allen

Newspapers, if they are to be interesting, must not be molested.

Frederick the Great

Harmony seldom makes a headline.

Silas Bent

What this generation was bred to at television's knees was not wisdom but cynicism.

Pauline Kael

The press is our chief ideological weapon. Its duty is to strike down the enemies of the working class.

Nikita Khrushchev

A people without reliable news is, sooner or later, a people without the basis of freedom.

Harold J. Laski

A journalist is a grumbler, a censurer, a giver of advice, a regent of sovereigns, a tutor of nations. Four hostile newspapers are more to be feared than a thousand bayonets.

Napoleon Bonaparte

The one function that TV news performs very well is that when there is no news we give it to you with the same emphasis as if there was news.

David Brinkley

I can get a better grasp of what is going on in the world from one good Washington dinner party than from all the background information NBC piles on my desk.

Barbara Walters

The newspapers! Sir, they are the most villainous—licentious—abominable—infernal— Not that I ever read them—no—I make it a rule never to look into a newspaper.

Richard Sheridan

He who first shortened the labor of Copyists by device of Movable Types was disbanding hired Armies and cashiering most Kings and Senates, and creating a whole new Democratic world: he had invented the Art of printing.

Thomas Carlyle

Middle Class

The most perfect political community is one in which the middle class is in control, and outnumbers both of the other classes.

Aristotle

A moderately honest man with a moderately faithful wife, moderate drinkers both, in a moderately healthy house: that is the true middle-class unit.

George Bernard Shaw

This picture of a despotic God who wants unrestricted power over men and their submission and humiliation was the projection of the middle class's own hostility and envy.

Erich Fromm

The Communist pie is nothing but crust. In America we have an upper crust and a lower crust, but it's what's between—the middle class—that gives the real flavor.

Virginia L. McCleary

The one class you do *not* belong to and are not proud of at all is the lower-middle class. No one ever describes himself as belonging to the lower-middle class.

George Mikes

The middle class is always a firm champion of equality when it concerns a class above it; but it is its inveterate foe when it concerns elevating a class below it.

Orestes A. Brownson

For a lot of middle-class women in this country, Women's Liberation is a matter of concern. For women on welfare, it's a matter of survival.

Johnnie Tillmon

Military

War is much too serious a thing to be left to military men.

C. M. Talleyrand

The necessary and wise subordination of the military to civil power [must] be sustained.

Dwight D. Eisenhower

The weakness of democracies is that once a general has been built up in public opinion it becomes impossible to remove him.

Édouard Daladier

If there is one basic element in our Constitution, it is civilian control of the military.

Harry S Truman

The military and not the civilian authorities should be in charge of nuclear weapons.

Edwin A. Walker

Thank heaven for the military-industrial complex. Its ultimate aim is peace for our time.

Barry Goldwater

In the councils of government we must guard against the acquisition of unwarranted influence, whether sought or unsought, by the military-industrial complex.

Dwight D. Eisenhower

In the choice of a general, we should regard his skill rather than his virtue—for few have military skill, but many have virtue.

Aristotle

Military intelligence is a contradiction in terms.

Groucho Marx

I never expect a soldier to think.

George Bernard Shaw

You cannot organize militarism and at the same time expect reason to control human destinies.

Franklin D. Roosevelt

One bad general is better than two good ones.

French saying

There is, then, over the affairs of the army a universal conspiracy of silence, of childlike mysteries, of clannishness, routine, and intrigue.

Jean Jaurès

Generals should mess with the common soldiers. The Spartan system was a good one.

Napoleon Bonaparte

And, as everyone knows, the army is a poor training corps for democracy no matter how inspiring the cause.

Pierre Trudeau

Peace is only too apt to lower the reputation of men that have grown great by arms, who naturally find difficulty in adapting themselves to the habits of civil equality.

Plutarch

A good general not only sees the way to victory; he also knows when victory is impossible.

Polybius

Military justice is to justice what military music is to music.

Groucho Marx

The spirit of this country is totally adverse to a large military force.

Thomas Jefferson

No nation ever had an army large enough to guarantee it against attack in time of peace or insure it victory in time of war.

Calvin Coolidge

Minorities

All history is a record of the power of minorities, and of minorities of one.

Ralph Waldo Emerson

A government is free in proportion to the rights it guarantees to the minority.

Alfred Landon

Governments exist to protect the rights of minorities.

Wendell Phillips

How a minority,
Reaching a majority,
Seizing authority,
Hates a minority!

Leonard H. Robbins

It is hell to belong to a suppressed minority. . . .

Claude McKay

Heresy is what the minority believe; it is the name given by the powerful to the doctrine of the weak.

Robert G. Ingersoll

Shall we judge a country by the majority, or by the minority? By the minority, surely.

Ralph Waldo Emerson

No democracy can long survive which does not accept as fundamental to its very existence the recognition of the rights of minorities.

Franklin D. Roosevelt

Ten people who speak make more noise than ten thousand who are silent.

Napoleon Bonaparte

Monarchy

The first king was a fortunate soldier.

Voltaire

That the king can do no wrong is a necessary and fundamental principle of the English Constitution.

William Blackstone

Kings are for nations in their swaddling clothes.

Victor Hugo

The Americans equally detest the pageantry of a king and the supercilious hypocrisy of a bishop.

Junius

Kings are happy in many things, but mainly in this: that they can do and say whatever they please.

Sophocles

Knowing the difficulties of a monarchy, I thank heaven I am spared being an absolute one.

George V

Republics come to an end by luxurious habits; monarchies by poverty.

C. S. Montesquieu

The trappings of a monarchy would set up an ordinary commonwealth.

Samuel Johnson

In a few years there will be only five kings in the world—the King of England and the four kings in a pack of cards.

King Farouk

Scratch a king and find a fool.

Dorothy Parker

When the king is said to be a good fellow, his reign is a failure.

Napoleon Bonaparte

My people and I have come to an agreement which satisfies us both. They are to say what they please, and I am to do what I please.

Frederick the Great

Abdication, n. An act whereby a sovereign attests his sense of the high temperature of the throne.

Ambrose Bierce

All kings is mostly rapscallions.

Huckleberry Finn

It has been said, not truly, but within a possible approximation of truth, that in 1802 every hereditary monarch was insane.

Walter Bagehot

The king reigns, but does not govern.

Jan Zamojski

The right divine of kings to govern wrong.

Alexander Pope

The King is one who has few things to desire and many things to fear.

Francis Bacon

Kings will be tyrants from policy, when subjects are rebels from principle.

Edmund Burke

Kings govern by popular assemblies only when they cannot do without them.

Charles Fox

In a monarchy the king must by necessity be above the law.
Robert Filmer

No state shall . . . grant any title of nobility.
Article I, U.S. Constitution, 1787

Money

Money is the mother's milk of politics.

Jesse Unruh

Money, the sinews of war.

Cicero

You may raise money enough to tunnel a mountain, but you cannot raise money enough to hire a man who is minding his own business.

Henry David Thoreau

The entire essence of America is the hope to first make money—then make money with money—then make lots of money with lots of money.

Paul Erdman

There are few ways in which a man can be more innocently employed than in getting money.

Samuel Johnson

Money is a new form of slavery, and distinguishable from the old simply by the fact that it is impersonal—that there is no human relations between master and slave.

Tolstoi

Money is the most egalitarian force in society. It confers power on whoever holds it.

Roger Starr

Money is like manure. You have to spread it around or it smells.

J. Paul Getty

It is the higher accomplishment to use money well than to use arms; but not to need it is more noble than to use it.

Plutarch

The more money an American accumulates, the less interesting he becomes.

Gore Vidal

Make money, money by fair means if you can, if not, by any means money.

Horace

It is physically impossible for a well-educated intellectual or brave man to make money the chief object of his thoughts.

John Ruskin

Where there is money, there is fighting.

Marian Anderson

The price we have to pay for money is paid in liberty.

Robert Louis Stevenson

Public money is like holy water; everyone helps himself.

Italian saying

He who has money has in his pocket those who have none.

Tolstoi

If all the rich men in the world divided up their money amongst themselves there wouldn't be enough to go around.

Jules Bertillon

Money is always there but the pockets change; it is not in the same pockets after a change, and that is all there is to say about money.

Gertrude Stein

There is a certain Buddhistic calm that comes from having . . . money in the bank.

Tom Robbins

If you can count your money, you don't have a billion dollars.

J. Paul Getty

Thrift is the great fortune maker. It draws the line between the savage and the civilized man.

Andrew Carnegie

Lack of money is the root of all evil.

George Bernard Shaw

We all know how the size of sums of money appears to vary in a remarkable way according as they are being paid in or paid out.

Julian Huxley

All currency is neurotic currency.

Norman O. Brown

Monopoly

Monopoly is business at the end of its journey.

Henry Demarest Lloyd

It is not competition, but monopoly, that deprives labor of its product.

Benjamin R. Tucker

Monopoly . . . is a great enemy to good management which can never be universally established but in consequence of that free and universal competition which forces everybody to have recourse to it for the sake of self-defense.

Adam Smith

Earnest attention should be given to those combinations of capital commodity commonly called Trusts.

Benjamin Harrison

. . . under a monopolistic economic system the opportunity to earn a living by one's labour comes to be regarded as a privilege instead of a natural right. Women are simply held to be less entitled to this privilege than men.

Suzanne LaFollette

If all I'm offered is a choice between monopolistic privilege with regulation and monopolistic privilege without regulation, I'm afraid I have to opt for the former.

Nicholas Johnson

The men who run the global corporations are the first in history with the organization, technology, money, and ideology to make a credible try at managing the world as an integrated unit.

Richard Barnet and Ronald Müller

No one can argue that a monopolist is impelled by "an invisible hand" to serve the public interest.

Richard Tawney

Strife is increasing in our times because true competition is diminishing.

John Bates Clark

Nationalism

If we have to start over again with another Adam and Eve, I want them to be Americans.

Richard Russell

A nation is a society united by a delusion about its ancestry and by a common hatred of its neighbors.

William R. Inge

Nationalism is an infantile disease. It is the measles of mankind.

Albert Einstein

Born in iniquity and conceived in sin, the spirit of nationalism has never ceased to bend human institutions to the service of dissension and distress.

Thorstein Veblen

I love my country too much to be a nationalist.

Albert Camus

Nationalism is our form of incest, is our idolatry, is our insanity. "Patriotism" is its cult.

Erich Fromm

Italy is a geographical expression.

Metternich

Our age is the age of the nationalization of intellect in political hatreds.

Julien Benda

The U.S. is having the same trouble as Rome in its search for "defensible frontiers."

Lord Curzon

Nation: a group of men who speak one language and read the same newspapers.

Friedrich Nietzsche

If there be a God, I think he would like me to paint Africa British-Red as possible.

Cecil Rhodes

Nations, like men, have their infancy.

Henry St. John

The efficiency of the truly national leader consists primarily in preventing the division of the attention of a people, and always in concentrating it on a single enemy.

Adolf Hitler

Neutrality

Armed neutrality.

Woodrow Wilson

The statesmanship of neutralism is the statesmanship of the tight-rope walker.

Max Lerner

Neutrals never dominate events. They always sink. Blood alone moves the wheels of history.

Benito Mussolini

That expression "positive neutrality" is a contradiction in terms. There can be no more positive neutrality than there can be a vegetarian tiger.

V. K. Krishna Menon

Nuclear

The best way not to use nuclear weapons is to be prepared to use them.

Samuel S. Stratton

All the wastes in a year from a nuclear power plant could be stored under a desk.

Ronald Reagan

If nuclear power plants are safe, let the commercial insurance industry insure them. Until those most expert judges of risk are willing to gamble with their money, I'm not willing to gamble with the health and safety of my family.

Donna Reed

How is it possible to practice restraint or selectivity with a weapon which wipes out cities with one blow?

Martin Buber

Man now has the power to put an end to his own history.

Thomas E. Murray

No annihilation without representation!

Arnold Toynbee

This atomic bomb is the Second Coming in Wrath.

Winston Churchill

The way to win an atomic war is to make certain it never starts.

Omar Bradley

Mankind must put an end to war, or war will put an end to mankind.

John F. Kennedy

The Atomic Age is here to stay—but are we?

Bennett Cerf

You're an old-timer if you can remember when setting the world on fire was a figure of speech.

Franklin P. Jones

Some day scientists may have the existence of mankind in its power, and the human race can commit suicide by blowing up the world.

Brooks Adams

It would be madness to let the purpose or the methods of private enterprise set the habits of the age of atomic energy.

Harold J. Laski

There is no local defense which alone will contain the mighty land power of the Communist world. Local defense must be reinforced by the further deterrent of massive retaliatory power.

John Foster Dulles

What difference does it make to the dead . . . whether the mad destruction is wrought under the name of totalitarianism or the holy name of liberty or democracy?

Mohandas Gandhi

I had a discussion with my daughter Amy the other day before I came here to ask her what the most important issue was. She said she thought nuclear weaponry and the control of nuclear arms.

Jimmy Carter

Give me the order to do it and I can break up Russia's five A-bomb nests in a week. And when I go up to meet Christ . . . I think I could explain to Him that I had saved civilization.

Orvil A. Anderson

Perhaps my dynamite plants will put an end to war sooner than your congresses. On the day two army corps can annihilate each other in one second all civilized nations will recoil from war in horror.

Alfred Nobel

The real war will never get in the books.

Walt Whitman

Pacifism

Sometime they'll give a war and nobody will come.

Carl Sandburg

We're not really pacifists, we're just nonviolent soldiers.

Joan Baez

I am an uncompromising pacifist. . . . I have no sense of nationalism, only a cosmic consciousness of belonging to the human family.

Rosika Schwimmer

The absolute pacifist is a bad citizen; times come when force must
be used to uphold right, justice and ideals.

Alfred North Whitehead

Nonviolence is not a garment to be put on and off at will. Its seat is
in the heart, and it must be an inseparable part of our being.

Mohandas Gandhi

That's all nonviolence is—organized love.

Joan Baez

Party

Party is the madness of many, for the gain of a few.

Robert Louis Stevenson

Party is organized opinion.

Benjamin Disraeli

Under democracy one party always devotes its chief energies to trying to prove that the other party is unfit to rule—and both commonly succeed, and are right.

H. L. Mencken

All political parties die at last of swallowing their own lies.

John Arbuthnot

When people agree on certain political ideas and want the power to put them into practice, they organize and call it a political party.

Saul Alinsky

Party is the historical organ by means of which a class becomes class conscious.

Leon Trotsky

The party permits ordinary people to get ahead. Without the party, I couldn't be a mayor.

Richard Daley

Parties seldom follow their best men. They follow their average sense.

Thomas B. Reed

Recollect that you were not made for the party, but the party for you.

H. H. Brackenridge

Damn your principles! Stick to your party.

Benjamin Disraeli

A party of order or stability, and a party of progress or reform, are both necessary elements of a healthy state of political life.

John Stuart Mill

All parties without exception, when they seek for power, are varieties of absolutism.

P. J. Proudhon

Patriotism

Our country is the world—our countrymen are all mankind.

William Lloyd Garrison

Our country! In her intercourse with foreign nations may she always be right; but our country, right or wrong.

Stephen Decatur

My country right or wrong, is a thing no patriot would think of saying except in a desperate case. It's like saying, "My mother, drunk or sober!"

G. K. Chesterton

That pernicious sentiment, "Our country, right or wrong."

James Russell Lowell

Our country . . . when right, to be kept right; when wrong, to be put right.

Carl Schurz

Patriotism is the passion of fools and the most foolish of passions.

Arthur Schopenhauer

At the bottom of all patriotism is war: that is why I am no patriot.

Jules Renard

Patriotism is a kind of religion: it is the egg from which wars are hatched.

Guy de Maupassant

Patriotism is the willingness to kill and be killed for trivial reasons.

Bertrand Russell

Patriotism, n. Combustible rubbish ready to the torch of any one ambitious to illuminate his name.

Ambrose Bierce

Patriotism is the last refuge of a scoundrel.

Samuel Johnson

In the great fulfillment we must have a citizenship less concerned about what the government can do for it and more anxious about what it can do for the nation.

Warren G. Harding

And so, my fellow Americans, ask not what your country can do for you; ask what you can do for your country.

John F. Kennedy

Ask not what you can do for your country, for they are liable to tell you.

Mark Steinbeck

Do not . . . regard the critics as questionable patriots. What were Washington and Jefferson and Adams but profound critics of the colonial status quo.

Adlai Stevenson

To me, it seems a dreadful indignity to have a soul controlled by geography.

George Santayana

If man commits suicide, it will be . . . because they will obey the clichés of state sovereignty and national honor.

Erich Fromm

Patriotism is your conviction that this country is superior to all other countries because you were born in it.

George Bernard Shaw

Patriotism is often an arbitrary veneration of real estate above principles.

George Jean Nathan

Patriotism has become a mere national assertion, a sentimentality of flag-cheering with no constructive duties.

H. G. Wells

Patriotism is as fierce as a fever, pitiless as the grave, blind as a stone and irrational as a headless man.

Ambrose Bierce

My rackets are run on strictly American lines and they're going to stay that way.

Al Capone

Patriotism is the virtue of the vicious.

Oscar Wilde

For us, patriotism is the same as the love of humanity.

Mohandas Gandhi

Whoever serves his country well has no need for ancestors.

Voltaire

Love for one's country which is not part of one's love for humanity is not love, but idolatrous worship.

Erich Fromm

Patriotism, to be truly American, begins with the human intelligence.

Norman Cousins

True patriotism doesn't exclude an understanding of the patriotism of others.

Elizabeth II

Patriotism may be defined as a sense of partisan solidarity in respect of prestige.

Thorstein Veblen

No other factor in history, not even religion, has produced so many wars as has the clash of national egotisms sanctified by the name of patriotism.

Preserved Smith

When a bishop at the first shot abandoned the worship of Christ and rallies his flock round the altar of Mars, he may be acting patriotically . . . but that does not justify him in pretending . . . that Christ, is, in effect, Mars.

George Bernard Shaw

As religion is imitated and mocked by hypocrisy, so public duty is parodied by patriotism.

J. E. Thorold Rogers

I should be able to love my country and love justice.

Albert Camus

The Athenian democracy suffered much from that narrowness of patriotism which is the ruin of all nations.

H. G. Wells

Patriotism is a praiseworthy competition with one's ancestors.

Tacitus

Patriotism corrupts history.

Johann Goethe

When a dog barks at the moon, then it is religion; but when he barks at strangers, it is patriotism.

David Starr Jordan

I only regret that I have but one life to lose for my country.

Nathan Hale

Patriotism is easy to understand in America. It means looking out for yourself by looking out for your country.

Calvin Coolidge

I realize that patriotism is not enough. I must have no hatred or bitterness towards anyone.

Edith Louise Cavell

Many studies have discovered a close link between prejudices and "patriotism." . . . Extreme bigots are almost always superpatriots.

Gordon W. Allport

. . . schools are out to teach patriotism; newspapers are out to stir up excitement; and politicians are out to get re-elected. None of the three, therefore, can do anything whatever toward saving the human race from reciprocal suicide.

Bertrand Russell

Peace

The wolf . . . shall dwell with the lamb, and the leopard shall lie down with the kid; and the calf and the young lion and the fatling together; and a little child shall lead them.

Isaiah 11:6

To find security without fighting is the acme of skill.

Sun-tzu

I believe it is peace for our time . . . peace with honor.

Neville Chamberlain

A peace which depends upon fear is nothing but a suppressed war.

Henry David Thoreau

Peace, n. In international affairs, a period of cheating between two periods of fighting.

Ambrose Bierce

Peace is a moribund condition, caused by a surplus of citizens which war seeks to remedy.

Cyril Connolly

Peace is much more precious than a piece of land.

Anwar el-Sadat

If I must choose between peace and righteousness, I choose righteousness.

Theodore Roosevelt

The most disadvantageous peace is better than the most just war.

Tacitus

It must be peace without victory.

Woodrow Wilson

They preferred victory to peace.

Tacitus

Again and again we have owed peace to the fact that we were prepared for war.

Theodore Roosevelt

To robbery, slaughter, plunder, they [the Romans] give the lying name of empire; they make a desolation and call it peace.

Tacitus

If man does find the solution for world peace it will be the most revolutionary reversal of his record we have ever known.

George C. Marshall

Peace is not only better than war, but infinitely more arduous.

George Bernard Shaw

We need to devise a system within which peace will be more rewarding than war.

Margaret Mead

The only way to abolish war [is] to make peace heroic.

John Dewey

Glory to God in the highest, and on earth peace, good will toward men.

Luke 2:14

Politician

He knows nothing; he thinks he knows everything—that clearly points to a political career.

George Bernard Shaw

. . . that insidious and crafty animal, vulgarly called a statesman or politician, whose councils are directed by momentary fluctuations of affairs.

Adam Smith

The politician is an acrobat. He keeps his balance by saying the opposite of what he does.

Maurice Barrès

Acting is as old as mankind. . . . Politicians are actors of the first order.

Marlon Brando

You have all the characteristics of a popular politician: a horrible voice, bad breeding and a vulgar manner.

Aristophanes

A statesman is a successful politician who is dead.

Thomas B. Reed

Now I know what a statesman is; he's a dead politician. We need more statesmen.

Bob Edwards

A statesman is any politician it's considered safe to name a school after.

Bill Vaughan

The more I see of the representatives of the people, the more I admire my dogs.

Alphonse de Lamartine

With the rashness of ignorance the uninitiated dare to dabble in affairs of state.

John of Salisbury

Fate often makes up for the eminence by the inferiority of the officeholder.

Baltasar Gracián

Men play at being God, but lacking God's experience they wind up as politicians.

Harry William King

A politician is one that would circumvent God.

William Shakespeare

Politics are too serious a matter to be left to politicians.

Charles de Gaulle

Mothers all want their sons to grow up to be President, but they didn't want them to become politicians in the process.

John F. Kennedy

The first method for estimating the intelligence of a ruler is to look at the men he has around him.

Niccolò Machiavelli

He brings disaster upon his nation who never sows a seed, or lays a brick, or weaves a garment, but makes politics his profession.

Kahlil Gibran

Now and then an innocent man is sent to the legislature.

Kin Hubbard

The most successful politician is he who says what everybody is thinking most often and in the loudest voice.

Theodore Roosevelt

Idealism is the noble toga that political gentlemen drape over their will to power.

Aldous Huxley

Public interest is a term used by every politician to support his ideas.

W. M. Kiplinger

The mules of politics: without pride of ancestry, or hope of posterity.

John O'Connor Power

Timid and interested politicians think much more about the security of their seats than about the security of their country.

Thomas Macaulay

Among politicians the esteem of religion is profitable; the principles of it are troublesome.

Benjamin Whichcote

To be a chemist you must study chemistry; to be a lawyer or a physician you must study law or medicine; but to be a politician you need only to study your own interests.

Max O'Rell

An important art of politicians is to find new names for institutions which under old names have become odious to the public.

C. M. Talleyrand

It is inexcusable for scientists to torture animals; let them make their experiments on journalists and politicians.

Henrik Ibsen

There is no worse heresy than that the office sanctifies the holder of it.

Lord Acton

Politics

Politics is perhaps the only profession for which no preparation is thought necessary.

Robert Louis Stevenson

Professional politicians like to talk about the value of experience in government. Nuts! The only experience you gain in politics is how to be political.

Ronald Reagan

One of the principal qualifications for a political job is that the applicant know nothing much about what he is expected to do.

Terry M. Townsend

Politics is the science of how who gets what, when and why.

Sidney Hillman

I am unsuited to politics since I am unable to wish for or accept my opponents' death.

Albert Camus

Practical politics consist in ignoring facts.

Henry Adams

Nothing is so admirable in politics as a short memory.

John Kenneth Galbraith

Being in politics is like being a football coach. You have to be smart enough to understand the game and dumb enough to think it's important.

Eugene McCarthy

In politics as on the sickbed people toss from one side to the other thinking they will be more comfortable.

Johann Goethe

Politics is the art of preventing people from busying themselves with what is their own business.

Paul Valéry

Politics makes strange bedfellows.

Charles Dudley

Politics makes strange bedfellows rich.

Wayne G. Haisley

Politics makes strange postmasters.

Kin Hubbard

What is politics but persuading the public to vote for this and support that and endure these for the promise of those.

Gilbert Highet

Politics should be the part-time profession of every citizen.

Dwight D. Eisenhower

Politics, n. A strife of interests masquerading as a contest of principles. The conduct of public affairs for private advantage.

Ambrose Bierce

Politics is the science of exigencies.

Theodore Parker

Politics is not an exact science.

Otto von Bismarck

You cannot adopt politics as a profession and remain honest.

Louis McHenry Howe

Politics ruins the character.

Otto von Bismarck

In politics there is no honour.

Benjamin Disraeli

Politics are nothing more than a means of rising in the world.

Samuel Johnson

"Practical politics" means selfish ends promoted by base means.

Rutherford B. Hayes

In politics, what begins in fear usually ends in folly.

Samuel Taylor Coleridge

In politics, an absurdity is not an impediment.

Napoleon Bonaparte

You in America should trust to that volcanic political instinct which I have divined in you.

George Bernard Shaw

Politics are almost as exciting as war, and quite as dangerous. In war you can only be killed once, but in politics many times.

Winston Churchill

If I had engaged in politics, O men of Athens, I should have perished long ago, and done no good either to you or to myself.

Socrates

The practice of politics in the East may be defined by one word—dissimulation.

Benjamin Disraeli

Or to some coffee-house I stray,
For news, the manna of a day,
And from the hipp'd discourses gather
That politics go by the weather.

Matthew Green

Politics, like religion, hold up the torches of martyrdom to the reformers of error.

Thomas Jefferson

Man is by nature a political animal.

Aristotle

The first mistake in public business is the going into it.

Benjamin Franklin

Poverty

No society can surely be flourishing and happy of which the far greater part of the members are poor and miserable.

Adam Smith

Of all the preposterous assumptions of humanity over humanity, nothing exceeds most of the criticisms made on the habits of the poor by the well-housed, well-warmed, and well-fed.

Herman Melville

The conspicuously wealthy turn up urging the character-building value of privation for the poor.

John Kenneth Galbraith

Every stable government in history has depended on the resignation of the poor to being poor.

Félicité de Lamennais

Must the hunger become anger and anger fury before anything will be done?

John Steinbeck

Poverty is the parent of revolution and crime.

Aristotle

Poverty in the United States is a culture, an institution, a way of life.

Michael Harrington

America is an enormous frosted cupcake in the middle of millions of starving people.

Gloria Steinem

The worst country to be poor in is America.

Arnold Toynbee

Poverty has, in large cities, very different appearances: it is often concealed in splendor, and often in extravagances.

Samuel Johnson

For any city, however small, is in fact divided into two, one the city of the poor, the other of the rich; these are at war with one another.

Plato

You don't have to look for distress; it is screaming at you.

Samuel Beckett

Wealth is conspicuous, but poverty hides.

James Reston

This administration, today, here and now, declares unconditional war on poverty in America.

Lyndon B. Johnson

War on nations changes maps. War on poverty maps change.

Muhammad Ali

Very few people can afford to be poor.

George Bernard Shaw

Poverty is expensive to maintain.

Michael Harrington

If a free society cannot help the many who are poor, it cannot save the few who are rich.

John F. Kennedy

A decent provision for the poor is the true test of civilization.

Samuel Johnson

Poverty does not produce unhappiness; it produces degradation.

George Bernard Shaw

Poverty destroys pride. It is difficult for an empty bag to stand up-right.

Alexandre Dumas, fils

Whereas it has long been known and declared that the poor have no right to the property of the rich, I wish it also to be known and declared that the rich have no right to the property of the poor.

John Ruskin

Poverty must have many satisfactions, else there would not be so many poor people.

Don Herold

An empty stomach is not a good political advisor.

Albert Einstein

That amid our highest civilization men faint and die with want is not due to the niggardliness of nature, but to the injustice of man.

Henry George

A hungry man is not a free man.

Adlai Stevenson

If the unemployed could eat plans and promises they would be able to spend the winter on the Riviera.

W.E.B. Du Bois

Pauperism is the hospital of the labor army.

Karl Marx

I think I have sufficient witness that I speak the truth, namely, my poverty.

Socrates

Most of our realists and sociologists talk about a poor man as if he were an octopus or an alligator.

G. K. Chesterton

Modern poverty is not the poverty that was blest in the Sermon on the Mount.

George Bernard Shaw

Laws grind the poor, and rich men rule the law.

Oliver Goldsmith

The critics were asking that we postpone consideration for the causes of poverty until no one was poor.

John Kenneth Galbraith

Half the world knows not how the other half lives.

George Herbert

Power

Politics are always a struggle for power, disguised and modified by prudence, reason and moral pretext.

William H. Mallock

As wealth is power, so all power will infallibly draw wealth to itself by some means or other.

Edmund Burke

Political power is merely the organized power of one class to oppress another.

Karl Marx

Power is always gradually stealing away from the many to the few, because the few are more vigilant and consistent.

Samuel Johnson

I have never been able to conceive how any rational being could propose happiness to himself from the exercise of power over others.

Thomas Jefferson

Political power grows out of the barrel of a gun.

Mao Zedong

No extraordinary power should be lodged in any one individual.

Thomas Paine

No one with absolute power can be trusted to give it up even in part.

Louis D. Brandeis

Those in power want only to perpetuate it.

William O. Douglas

Power tends to corrupt; absolute power corrupts absolutely.

Lord Acton

Unlimited power is apt to corrupt the minds of those who possess it.

William Pitt, the Younger

Freedom is participation in power.

Cicero

Even weak men when united are powerful.

J.C.F. von Schiller

Power always has to be kept in check; power exercised in secret, especially under the cloak of *national security*, is doubly dangerous.

William Proxmire

The most dangerous form of inebriation results from too much power.

Frank Tyger

He who makes another powerful ruins himself, for he makes the other so either by shrewdness or force, and both of these qualities are feared by the one who becomes powerful.

Niccolò Machiavelli

The only prize much cared for by the powerful is power. The prize of the general is not a bigger tent, but command.

Oliver Wendell Holmes, Jr.

It is a strange desire to seek power and to lose liberty.

Francis Bacon

Power gradually extirpates from the mind every humane and gentle virtue.

Edmund Burke

The way to have power is to take it.

W. M. Tweed

The measure of man is what he does with power.

Pittacus

The reputation of power *is* power.

Thomas Hobbes

Power is more retained by wary measures than by daring counsels.

Tacitus

The shortest way to ruin a country is to give power to demagogues.

Dionysius

Man is born to seek power, yet his actual condition makes him a slave to the power of others.

Hans J. Morgenthau

The love of liberty is the love of others; the love of power is the love of ourselves.

William Hazlitt

We have, I fear, confused power with greatness.

Stewart L. Udall

Presidency

The executive power shall be vested in a President of the United States of America. He shall hold his office during the term of four years.

Article III, U.S. Constitution, 1787

When I was a boy I was told that anybody could become President; I'm beginning to believe it.

Clarence Darrow

When we got into office, the thing that surprised me most was to find that things were just as bad as we'd been saying they were.

John F. Kennedy

Once upon a time my political opponents honored me as possessing the fabulous intellectual and economic power by which I created a worldwide depression all by myself.

Herbert Hoover

No man will ever bring out of the Presidency the reputation which carries him into it.

Thomas Jefferson

In America any boy may become President and I suppose it's just one of the risks he takes.

Adlai Stevenson

I am a man of limited talents from a small town. I don't seem to grasp that I am President.

Warren G. Harding

I sit here all day trying to persuade people to do the things they ought to have sense enough to do without my persuading them. That's all the powers of the President amount to.

Harry S Truman

When the President says "jump" they only ask, "How high?"

John Ehrlichman

The power to blow up the world cannot be entrusted to anyone sick enough to seek it.

Philip Slater

The Presidency is mysterious because it is formidable; mystery is inherent in power.

Richard H. Rovere

A man who is influenced by the polls or is afraid to make decisions which may make him unpopular is not a man to represent the welfare of the country.

Harry S Truman

I would rather be right than President.

Henry Clay

I know that when things don't go well they like to blame the Presidents and that is one of the things which Presidents are paid for. . . .

John F. Kennedy

When a man has cast his longing eye on offices, a rottenness begins in his conduct.

Thomas Jefferson

You are apprehensive of monarchy; I, of aristocracy. I would therefore have given more power to the President and less to the Senate.

John Adams

Presidency, n. The greased pig in the field game of American politics.

Ambrose Bierce

Seen one President, you've seen them all.

Henry Kissinger

How can you govern a nation that has two hundred and forty-six different kinds of cheese?

Charles de Gaulle

In the White House, the future rapidly becomes the past; and delay itself a decision.

Theodore Sorenson

I felt as if I had lived five lifetimes in my first five days as President.

Harry S Truman

It is the President's decision to choose how to impart information to the people

John Ehrlichman

The office of President is such a bastardized thing, half royalty and half democracy, that nobody knows whether to genuflect or spit.

Jimmy Breslin

I have been told I was on the road to hell, but I had no idea it was just a mile down the road with a Dome on it.

Abraham Lincoln

You can always get the truth from an American statesman after he has turned seventy or given up all hope of the Presidency.

Wendell Phillips

Being a President is like riding a tiger. A man has to keep on riding or be swallowed.

Harry S Truman

When a man assumes a public trust, he should consider himself a public property.

Thomas Jefferson

Though it would be safer for a President to live in a cage, it would interfere with his business.

Abraham Lincoln

If forced to choose between the penitentiary and the White House for four years, I would say the penitentiary, thank you.

William T. Sherman

Congress is very generous to the President. . . . I have been able to save from my four years about $100,000.

William H. Taft

If you are as happy, my dear sir, on entering this house as I am leaving it and returning home, you are the happiest man in this country.

James Buchanan

I should like to be known as a former President who minded his own business.

Calvin Coolidge

Oh, that lovely title, ex-President.

Dwight D. Eisenhower

The American Presidency, it occurs to us, is merely a way station en route to the blessed condition of being an ex-President.

John Updike

What a lousy, fucked-up job this turned out to be.

John F. Kennedy

Propaganda

Propaganda is the art of persuading others of what one does not believe oneself.

Abba Eban

There is no need for propaganda to be rich in intellectual content.

Joseph Paul Goebbels

A group is subject to the truly magical power of words.

Sigmund Freud

The great masses of the people . . . will more easily fall victims to a great lie than to a small one.

Adolf Hitler

Why is propaganda so much more successful when it stirs up hatred than when it tries to stir up friendly feeling?

Bertrand Russell

Each government accuses the other of perfidy, intrigue and ambition, as a means of heating the imagination of their respective nations, and incensing them to hostilities.

Thomas Paine

The Marine Corps is the Navy's police force and as long as I am President that is what it will remain. They have a propaganda machine that is almost equal to Stalin's.

Harry S Truman

Like the effect of advertising upon the customer, the methods of political propaganda tend to increase the feeling of insignificance of the individual voter.

Erich Fromm

The propagandist's purpose is to make one set of people forget that certain other sets of people are human.

Aldous Huxley

Propaganda is a soft weapon: hold it in your hands long, and it will move about like a snake, and strike the other way.

Jean Anouilh

It is the absolute right of the state to supervise the formation of public opinion.

Joseph Paul Goebbels

Journalism is not a profession but a mission. Our newspaper is our party, our ideal, our soul, and our banner which will lead us to victory.

Benito Mussolini

The press should be not only a collective propagandist and a collective agitator, but also a collective organizer of the masses.

Nikolai Lenin

In the midst of increasing mechanization and technological organization, propaganda is simply the means used to prevent these things from being felt as too oppressive and to persuade man to submit with good grace.

Jacques Ellul

. . . the propaganda arm of the American Dream machine, Hollywood . . .

Molly Haskell

History is the propaganda of the victors.

Ernest Toller

Property

In no country in the world is the love of property more active and more anxious than in the United States.

Alexis de Tocqueville

Democracy . . . began as a system which gave suffrage to those who had proved their worth by acquiring real property and to no other.

John Kenneth Galbraith

The reason why men enter into society is the preservation of their property.

John Locke

Private property is at once the consequence and the basis of the state.

Mikhail Bakunin

We stand for the maintenance of private property.

Adolf Hitler

Property exists by force of the law. It is not a fact, but a legal fiction.

Max Stirner

Civil government, so far as it is instituted for the security of property, is in reality instituted for the defence of the rich against the poor, or of those who have some property against those who have none at all.

Adam Smith

The first man who, having fenced in a piece of land, said "This is mine," and found people naive enough to believe him, that man was the true founder of civil society.

Jean Jacques Rousseau

Property is necessary, but it is not necessary that it should remain forever in the same hands.

Rémy de Gourmont

Property is not theft, but a good deal of theft becomes property.

Richard Tawney

Property . . . has been well compared to snow—"if it fall level to-day, it will be blown into drifts to-morrow."

Ralph Waldo Emerson

Private property . . . is the creature of society and is subject to the calls of that society even to the last farthing.

Benjamin Franklin

Every man holds his property subject to the general right of the community to regulate its use to whatever degree the public welfare may require it.

Theodore Roosevelt

In every society where property exists there will ever be a struggle between rich and poor. Mixed in one assembly, equal laws can never be expected; they will either be made by the members to plunder the few who are rich, or by the influential to fleece the many who are poor.

John Adams

The man who has half a million dollars in property . . . has a much higher interest in the government than the man who has little or no property.

Noah Webster

The interest of those who own property used in industry . . . is that their capital should be dear and human beings cheap.

Richard Tawney

By abolishing private property one deprives the human love of aggression.

Sigmund Freud

It is the preoccupation with possession, more than anything else, that prevents men from living freely and nobly.

Bertrand Russell

The balance of power in a society accompanies the balance of property in land.

John Adams

Property and law are born together, and die together.

Jeremy Bentham

In the last analysis the property-owning class is loyal only to its own property.

John Reed

Laws are always useful to persons of property, and hurtful to those who have none.

Jean Jacques Rousseau

Every man has by nature the right to possess property as his own.

Pope Leo XIII

In nature, exclusive property is theft.

J. P. Brissot

Public Opinion

Politicians, after all, are not a year behind Public Opinion.

Will Rogers

In America, public opinion is the leader.

Frances Perkins

Our government rests on public opinion. Whoever can change public opinion can change the government practically as such.

Abraham Lincoln

Public opinion is no more than this.
What people think that other people think.

Alfred Austin

That mysterious independent variable of political calculation, Public Opinion.

Thomas Huxley

Public opinion is the last refuge of a politician without any opinion.
Mark Bonham Carter

Public opinion is a compound of folly, weakness, prejudice, wrong feeling, right feeling, obstinacy and newspaper paragraphs.

Robert Peel

A straw vote only shows which way the hot air blows.

O. Henry

Opinion surveys are people who don't matter reporting on opinions that do matter.

John A. Lincoln

What the multitude says is so, or soon will be so.

Baltasar Gracián

The public buys its opinions as it buys its meats or takes its milk, on the principle that it is cheaper to do this than to keep a cow. So it is, but the milk is more likely to be watered.

Samuel Butler

Popular opinion, on subjects not palpable to sense, are often true, but seldom or never the whole truth.

John Stuart Mill

There are times when the belief of the people, though it may be without ground, is as significant as the truth.

J.C.F. von Schiller

A man's opinions are generally of much more value than his arguments.

Oliver Wendell Holmes, Jr.

Polls are like sleeping pills designed to lull the voters into sleeping on election day. You might call them "sleeping polls."

Harry S Truman

As force is always on the side of the governed, the governors have nothing to support them but opinion. It is, therefore, on opinion only that government is founded; and this maxim extends to the most despotic and most military governments, as well as to the most free and the most popular.

David Hume

Private opinion is weak, but public opinion is almost omnipotent.

Harriet Beecher Stowe

Laws that do not embody public opinion can never be enforced.

Elbert Hubbard

Public opinion's always in advance of the Law.

John Galsworthy

Public opinion is stronger than the legislature, and nearly as strong as the Ten Commandments.

Charles Dudley Warner

Circumstances are the creators of most men's opinions.

A. V. Dicey

. . . the coquetry of public opinion, which has her caprices, and must have her way.

Edmund Burke

It requires ages to destroy a popular opinion.

Voltaire

A universal feeling, whether well or ill founded, cannot be safely disregarded.

Abraham Lincoln

The foolish and the dead alone never change their opinion.

James Russell Lowell

Prejudice is an opinion without judgment.

Voltaire

Opinion is ultimately determined by the feelings, and not by the intellect.

Herbert Spencer

A plague of opinion! A man may wear it on both sides like a leather jerkin.

William Shakespeare

The people are a many-headed beast.

Alexander Pope

So many men, so many opinions.

Terence

Punishment

I agree with the death penalty. I think that people would be alive today if there were a death penalty.

Nancy Reagan

It is well-nigh obvious that those who are in favor of the death penalty have more affinities with murderers than those who oppose it.

Rémy de Gourmont

When we execute a murderer, it may be that we fall into the same mistake as the child that strikes a chair it has collided with.

G. C. Lichtenberg

Our criminal system is an organized attempt to produce white by two blacks.

Jean Jacques Rousseau

If a man destroy the eye of another man, they shall destroy his eye.
Hammurabi Code, ca. 2250 B.C.

He that smiteth a man, so that he die, shall be surely put to death.
Exodus 21;12

For a deadly blow let him pay with a deadly blow: it is for him who has done a deed to suffer.

Aeschylus

Let the punishment match the offense.

Cicero

Excessive bail shall not be required, nor excessive fines imposed, nor cruel and unusual punishment inflicted.

Seventh Amendment, U.S. Constitution, 1791

Hanging is the worst use man can be put to.

Henry Wotton

The punishment of criminals should serve a purpose. A hanged man is good for nothing. . . .

Voltaire

It is not the thief who is hanged, but one who was caught stealing.

Czechoslovakian saying

Men are not hanged for stealing horses, but that horses may not be stolen.

George Savile

A community is infinitely more brutalized by the helpful employment of punishment than it is by the occasional occurrence of crime.

Oscar Wilde

Capital punishment . . . has always been a religious punishment and is irreconcilable with humanism.

Albert Camus

Assassination on the scaffold is the worst form of assassination, because it is invested with the approval of society

George Bernard Shaw

Prisons are built with stones of Law, brothels with bricks of religion.

William Blake

There was never fair prison.

John Davies

While we have prisons it matters little which of us occupy the cells.

George Bernard Shaw

Under a government which imprisons any unjustly, the true place for a just man is also a prison.

Henry David Thoreau

Extreme justice is extreme injustice.

Cicero

Race

It's been a struggle for me because I had a chance to be white and I refused.

Richard Pryor

I believe in white supremacy until the blacks are educated to a point of responsibility.

John Wayne

You cannot have law and order and niggers, too.

J. B. Stoner

No niggah's good as a white man, because the niggah's only a few shawt yeahs from cannibalism.

Eugene Talmadge

Why would we have different races if God meant us to be alike and associate with each other?

Lester Maddox

. . . another Negro hung naked from a tree. In the background a Klansman held aloft a large American flag.

Jacob Javits

I happen to know quite a bit about the South. Spent twenty years there one night.

Dick Gregory

We are all descendants of Adam and we are all products of racial miscegenation.

Lester B. Pearson

Black is Beautiful.

Stokely Carmichael

We are the first race in the world, and the more of the world we inherit the better it is for the human race.

Cecil Rhodes

All who are not of good race in this world are chaff.

Adolf Hitler

There are many humorous things in the world, among them the white man's notion that he is less savage than the other savages.

Mark Twain

Whenever the Constitution comes between me and the virtue of white women of South Carolina, I say—to hell with the Constitution!

Coleman L. Blease

If you're white, you're right,
If you're black, stay back.

Black American saying

You can't hold a man down without staying down with him.

Booker T. Washington

Color is not human or personal reality; it is a political reality.

James Baldwin

The time may have come when the issue of race could benefit from a period of "benign neglect."

Daniel Patrick Moynihan

The "Negro problem" and the "white man's burden" are historical misnomers. The problem never was "Negro." The problem is . . . Caucasian, Anglo-Saxon, European, white.

John Oliver Killens

I am not an American. I am one of 22 million black people who are victims of Americanism.

Malcolm X

At first we had the land and the white man had the Bible. Now we have the Bible and the white man has the land.

Bantu Indian saying

This is the red man's country by natural right, and the black man's by virtue of his suffering and toil.

Robert Purvis

The Negro is the barometer of all American institutions and values.

Whitney Moore Young

The only good Indian I ever saw is a dead Indian.

Philip Sheridan

Many, if not most, of our Indian wars have had their origin in broken promises and acts of injustice on our part.

Rutherford B. Hayes

Radicalism

Radicalism is a label that is always applied to people who are endeavoring to get freedom.

Marcus Moziah Garvey

The radical of one century is the conservative of the next.

Mark Twain

The idealists and visionaries, foolish enough to throw caution to the winds and express their ardor and faith in some supreme deed, have advanced mankind and have enriched the world.

Emma Goldman

If a man is right he can't be too radical; if he is wrong, he can't be too conservative.

Henry Wheeler Shaw

Extremism in the defense of liberty is no voice. . . . Moderation in the pursuit of justice is no virtue.

Barry Goldwater

I can live with the robber barons, but how do you live with these pathological liars?

Daniel Patrick Moynihan

Radicalism, n. The conservatism of to-morrow injected into the affairs of to-day.

Ambrose Bierce

What this country needs is radicals who will stay that way regardless of the creeping years.

John Fisher

The healthy stomach is nothing if not conservative. Few radicals have good digestions.

Samuel Butler

Every reform movement has a lunatic fringe.

Theodore Roosevelt

Reactionary

All reactionaries are paper tigers.

Mao Zedong

I don't believe I have any moral justification for repudiating them [the John Birch Society].

Ronald Reagan

The more there are riots, the more repressive action will take place, and the more we face the danger of a right-wing take-over and eventually a fascist society.

Martin Luther King, Jr.

Any movement in history which attempts to perpetuate itself, becomes reactionary.

Tito

A reactionary is a somnambulist walking backward.

Franklin D. Roosevelt

Look at the John Birch society. Look at Hitler. The reactionaries are always better organized.

Cesar Chavez

New opinions are always suspected, and usually opposed, without any other reason but because they are not already common.

John Locke

Reactionaries must be deprived of the right to voice their opinions; only the people have that right.

Mao Zedong

Extremists think "communication" means agreeing with them.

Leo Rosten

Loyalty to a petrified opinion never yet broke a chain or freed a soul.

Mark Twain

No influence so quickly converts a radical into a reactionary as does his election to power.

Elisabeth Marbury

Reformers

A human being is happiest and most successful when dedicated to a
cause outside his own individual, selfish, satisfaction.

Benjamin Spock

To give up the task of reforming society is to give up one's responsibility as a free man.

Alan Paton

Those who have given themselves the most concern about the happiness of people have made their neighbors very miserable.

Anatole France

There are a thousand hacking at the branches of evil to one who is
striking at the root.

Henry David Thoreau

Unless the reformer can invent something which substitutes attractive virtues for attractive vices, he will fail.

Walter Lippmann

Attempts at reform, when they fail, strengthen despotism, as he
that struggles tightens the cords he does not succeed in breaking.

Charles C. Colton

Every man is a reformer until reform tramps on his toes.

E. W. Howe

The men who have changed the universe have never accomplished
it by changing officials but always by inspiring the people.

Napoleon Bonaparte

Every reform was once a private opinion, and when it shall be a private opinion again, it will solve the problem of the age.

Ralph Waldo Emerson

Religion

No politician has ever yet been able to rule his country, nor has any country ever yet been able to face the world, upon the principles of the Sermon on the Mount.

Frederick Scott Oliver

Material wealth is God's way of blessing people who put Him first.

Jerry Falwell

I know you can't endorse me. I want you to know that I endorse you [the Moral Majority].

Ronald Reagan

God would not be pleased if we return His creation to Him in ashes.

John Tursby

Religion is the sigh of the oppressed creature, the feelings of a heartless world and the spirit of conditions which are unspiritual. It is the opium of the people.

Karl Marx

Churches are suffered to exist only on condition that they preach submission to the State as at present capitalistically organized.

George Bernard Shaw

Democracy is itself a religious faith. For some it comes close to being the only formal religion they have.

E. B. White

It is ever thus; where Theology enchains the soul, the Tyrant enslaves the body.

Emily Collins

No one can claim to be called Christian who gives money for the building of warships and arsenals.

Belva Lockwood

You see few people here in America who really care very much about living a Christian life in a democratic world.

Clare Boothe Luce

The pious ones of Plymouth, who, reaching the Rock, first fell upon their knees and then upon the aborigines.

William M. Evarts

Congress shall make no law respecting an establishment of religion, or prohibiting the free exercise thereof.

First Amendment, U.S. Constitution, 1791

In the Papal System, Government and Religion are in a manner consolidated and that is found to be the worst of government.

James Madison

I believe in absolute separation of Church and State. . . . I believe in the support of the public school.

Calvin Coolidge

Render to Caesar the things that are Caesar's and to God the things that are God's.

Luke 12:17

The Church ought to be separated from the state, and the state from the Church.

Pope Pius IX

In all ages, hypocrites, called priests, have put crowns upon the heads of thieves, called kings.

Robert G. Ingersoll

The First Amendment has erected a wall between church and state. That wall must be kept high and impregnable. We could not approve the slightest breach.

Hugo L. Black

All religions united with government are more or less inimical to liberty. All, separated from government, are compatible with liberty.

Henry Clay

Theocracy, government of God, is precisely the thing to be struggled for.

Thomas Carlyle

The adulterous connection of church and state.

Thomas Paine

I believe that the outlawing of prayer in public schools is against the Constitution. This is a nation of God. It is still on our coin: In God We Trust.

Ronald Reagan

Recent discoveries down through the years have pointed up great flaws in it [evolution].

Ronald Reagan

The humblest citizen of all the land, when clad in the armor of a righteous cause, is stronger than all the hosts of error.

William Jennings Bryan

Nationality is often silly. Every nation believes that the Divine Providence has a sneaking kindness for it.

Ralph Waldo Emerson

We Americans have no commission from God to police the world.

Benjamin Harrison

I say the real and permanent grandeur of these States must be their religion.

Walt Whitman

God hath sifted a nation that he might send choice grain into this wilderness.

William Stoughton

It is for the good of states that men should be deluded by religion.

Varro

There is a higher law than the Constitution.

William H. Seward

There is a holy, mistaken zeal in politics, as well as religion. By persuading others we convince ourselves.

Junius

I rather think there is an immense shortage of Christian charity among so-called Christians.

Harry S Truman

America! America!
God shed His grace on thee.

Katherine Lee Bates

A nation must have a religion, and that religion must be under the control of the government.

Napoleon Bonaparte

In Russia religion is the opium of the people; in China opium is the religion of the people.

Edgar Snow

Religion is one of the forms of spiritual oppression which everywhere weigh upon the masses who are crushed by continuous toil for others, by poverty and loneliness.

Nikolai Lenin

My father was a Democrat; my mother was a Republican; I am an Episcopalian.

George C. Marshall

The day that this country ceases to be free for irreligion, it will cease to be free for religion.

Robert H. Jackson

Difference of religion breeds more quarrels than difference in politics.

Wendell Phillips

It is a reproach to religion and government to suffer so much poverty and excess.

William Penn

Nothing is more foreign to us Christians than politics.

Tertullian

Free government is the political expression of a deeply felt religious faith.

Dwight D. Eisenhower

Things have come to a pretty pass when religion is allowed to invade the sphere of private life.

William Lamb

I wished I could be a Catholic in Catholic countries, and a Protestant in Protestant ones.

Samuel Butler

All religions must be tolerated, and the sole concern of the authorities should be to see that one does not molest another, for here every man must be saved in his own way.

Frederick the Great

Religion is regarded by the common people as true, by the wise as false, and by the rulers as useful.

Seneca

Reproductive Rights

If men could get pregnant, abortion would be a sacrament.

Florynce R. Kennedy

Abortion is advocated only by persons who have themselves been born.

Ronald Reagan

For all Americans, and especially the poor, we must put an end to compulsory pregnancy.

Shirley Chisholm

No woman can call herself free who does not own and control her body.

Margaret Sanger

The loneliness, the sense of abandonment, of being imprisoned, powerless, and depersonalized is the chief collective memory of women who have given birth in American hospitals.

Adrienne Rich

Birth Control, therefore, means not merely the limitation of births, but the application of intelligent guidance over the reproductive power.

Margaret Sanger

No matter what men think, abortion is a fact of life. Women will have them; they always have and always will. Are they going to have good ones or bad ones? Will the good ones be reserved for the rich while poor women have to go to quacks?

Shirley Chisholm

If one is willing to have children, Rhythm is probably the best method of contraception.

Elizabeth Hawes

When legalized abortion is suggested the anti-abortionist immediately cries, "infanticide!" Yet his shrill voice is silent in the face of war. . . . Our society accepts war—a ritualized, institutionalized form of murder—and yet protests the removal of an unsentient cluster of cells.

Natalie Shainess

. . . how much cruel bondage of mind and suffering of body poor woman will escape when she takes the liberty of being her own physician of both body and soul.

Elizabeth Cady Stanton

Republican Party

The Republicans have a habit of having three bad years and one good one, and the good one always happens to be election years.

Will Rogers

The trouble with the Republican Party is that it has not had a new idea for thirty years.

Woodrow Wilson

Republicans are for both the man and the dollar, but in case of conflict the man before the dollar.

Abraham Lincoln

Every Republican candidate for President since 1936 has been nominated by the Chase National Bank.

Robert A. Taft

The people are wise—wiser than the Republicans think.

Adlai Stevenson

The Republican Convention [1928] opened with a prayer. If the Lord can see his way to bless the Republican Party the way it's been carrying on, then the rest of us ought to get it without even asking.

Will Rogers

The Republican Party either corrupts its liberals or it expels them.

Harry S Truman

The function of liberal Republicans is to shoot the wounded after battle.

Eugene McCarthy

The Republicans have their splits after the election and Democrats have theirs just before an election.

Will Rogers

Republicans no longer worship at the shrine of a balanced budget.

Jack Kemp

Revolution

Any person under the age of thirty, who, having any knowledge of the existing social order is not a revolutionist, is an inferior.

George Bernard Shaw

Whenever they shall grow weary of the existing government they can exercise their constitutional right of amending it, or their constitutional right to dismember or overthrow it.

Abraham Lincoln

Those who make peaceful revolution impossible will make violent revolution inevitable.

John F. Kennedy

The Revolution . . . is a dictatorship of the exploited against the exploiters.

Fidel Castro

We are not to expect to be translated from despotism to liberty in a featherbed.

Thomas Jefferson

Revolution, n. In politics, an abrupt change in the form of misgovernment.

Ambrose Bierce

You can jail a revolutionary, but you cannot jail the revolution.

Bobby Seale

If it takes a bloodbath, let's get it over with. No more appeasement.

Ronald Reagan

To be a revolutionary you have to be a human being. You have to care about people who have no power.

Jane Fonda

The true revolutionary is guided by a great feeling of love.

Che Guevara

A revolution is not a dinner party, or writing an essay, or painting a picture, or doing embroidery; it cannot be so refined.

Mao Zedong

God forbid we should ever be twenty years without such a rebellion.

Thomas Jefferson

The fundamental principle is that no battle, combat or skirmish is to be fought unless it will be won.

Che Guevara

The path that leads from moral standards to political activity is strewn with our dead selves.

André Malraux

The concessions of the privileged to the unprivileged are seldom brought about by any better motive than the power of the unprivileged to extort them.

John Stuart Mill

A populace never rebels from passion for attack, but from impatience of suffering.

Edmund Burke

Revolution by the Have-Nots has a way of inducing a moral revolution among the Haves.

Saul Alinsky

All civilization has from time to time become a thin crust over a volcano of revolution.

Havelock Ellis

Revolution is the festival of the oppressed.

Germaine Greer

The purity of a revolution can last a fortnight.

Jean Cocteau

Oppressed people are frequently very oppressive when first liberated. . . . They know best two positions. Somebody's foot on their neck or their foot on somebody's neck.

Florynce Kennedy

The Revolution is like Saturn—it eats its own children.

Georg Büchner

Revolutions are apt to take their color from the regime they overthrow.

Richard H. Tawney

Nothing is clearer in history than the adoption by successful rebels of the methods they were accustomed to condemn in the forces they deposed.

Will and Ariel Durant

Revolutions are not about trifles, but they are produced by trifles.

Aristotle

Old forms of government finally grow so oppressive that they must be thrown off even at the risk of reigns of terror.

Herbert Spencer

The government of a revolution is the despotism of liberty against tyranny.

Maximilien Robespierre

Repression is the seed of revolution.

Daniel Webster

An oppressed people are authorized, whenever they can, to rise and break their fetters.

Henry Clay

In this Revolution no plans have been written for retreat.

Martin Luther King, Jr.

Revolutions never go backward.

Wendell Phillips

To dare: that is the whole secret of revolution.

Antoine Saint-Just

It's a sad and stupid thing to have to proclaim yourself a revolution-ary just to be a decent man.

David Harris

Revolutions are not exportable.

Nikita Khrushchev

Every revolution is the consequence of one revolution and the be-ginning of another.

Chateaubriand

Revolution is but thought carried into action.

Emma Goldman

In politics experiments mean revolutions.

Benjamin Disraeli

The successful revolutionary is a statesman, the unsuccessful one a criminal.

Erich Fromm

No committee ever has, or ever will, run a revolution.

Annie Kenney

Not actual suffering but the hope of better things incites people to revolt.

Eric Hoffer

A revolution is coming—a revolution which will be peaceful if we are wise enough; compassionate if we care enough; successful if we are fortunate enough—but a revolution which is coming whether we will it or not. We can affect its character; we cannot alter its inevitability.

Robert F. Kennedy

Science

America's technology has turned in upon itself; its corporate form makes it the servant of profits, not the servant of human needs.

Alice Embree

Our scientific power has outrun our spiritual power. We have guided missiles and misguided men.

Martin Luther King, Jr.

If there is technological advance without social advance, there is, almost automatically, an increase in human misery.

Michael Harrington

Every time you scientists make a major invention, we politicians have to invent an institution to cope with it—and almost invariably, these days, it must be an international institution.

John F. Kennedy

At the end of the first half-century of engine-driven flight, we are confronted with the stark fact that the historical significance of aircraft has been primarily military and destructive.

Charles A. Lindbergh

The marvels of modern technology include the development of a soda can which, when discarded, will last forever—and a $7,000 car which, when properly cared for, will rust out in two or three years.

Paul Harwitz

Science is the greatest instrument of social change . . . the most vital of all revolutions which have marked the development of modern civilizations.

Arthur Balfour

Society produces technology and technology produces society in an endless mesh of action and interaction.

Kenneth E. Boulding

Scientists have it within them to know what a future-directed society feels like, for science itself, in its human aspect, is just that.

C. P. Snow

In some sort of crude sense which no vulgarity, no humor, no overstatement can quite extinguish, the physicists have known sin; and this is a knowledge which they cannot lose.

J. Robert Oppenheimer

Modern man worships at the temple of science, but science tells him only what is possible, not what is right.

Milton S. Eisenhower

Science and art belong to the whole world, and before them vanish the barriers of nationality.

Johann Goethe

If science could operate unchecked, it would soon produce a single world state.

Bertrand Russell

Every succeeding scientific discovery makes greater nonsense of old-time conceptions of sovereignty.

Anthony Eden

A tool is but the extension of a man's hand, and a machine is but a complex tool. He that invents a machine augments the power of a man and the well-being of mankind.

Henry Ward Beecher

Bourgeois scientists make sure that their theories are not dangerous to God or to capital.

Karl Marx

The world is dying of machinery; that is the great disease, that is the plague that will sweep away and destroy civilization; man will have to rise against it sooner or later.

George Moore

The evil that machinery is doing is not merely in the consequences of its work but in the fact that it makes men themselves machines also.

Oscar Wilde

The great tragedy of Science—the slaying of a beautiful hypothesis by an ugly fact.

Thomas Huxley

Science cannot bear the thought that there is an important natural phenomenon which it cannot hope to explain even with unlimited time and money.

Robert Johnson

Can we unlearn the arts that pretend to civilize, and then burn the world? There is a march of science; but who shall beat the drums for its retreat?

Charles Lamb

Slavery

If it wasn't for Abe, I'd still be on the open market.

Dick Gregory

The haughty American nation . . . makes the Negro clean its boots and then proves the moral and physical inferiority of the Negro by the fact that he is a bootblack.

George Bernard Shaw

Freedom has a thousand charms to show,
That slaves, howe'er contented, never know.

William Cowper

If you could just be a nigger one Saturday night, you wouldn't never want to be a white man again as long as you live.

William Faulkner

It seems almost incredible that the advocates of liberty should conceive the idea of selling a fellow creature to slavery.

James Forten

If you put a chain around the neck of a slave, the other end fastens itself around your own.

Ralph Waldo Emerson

Man is born free, yet he is everywhere in chains.

Jean Jacques Rousseau

The Man ain't prejudiced. He doesn't care what color his slaves are.

Chester Anderson

Slavery is an institution for converting men into monkeys.

Ralph Waldo Emerson

God wills us free, man wills us slaves,
I will as God wills, God's will be done.

Daniel Bliss

If they really believe there is danger from the Negro, it must be because they do not intend to give him justice.

Booker T. Washington

This country was formed for the white, not for the black man. And looking upon African slavery from the same viewpoint held by the noble framers of our Constitution, I for one have ever considered it one of the greatest blessings that God ever has bestowed upon a favored nation.

John Wilkes Booth

We must get rid of slavery or we must get rid of freedom.

Ralph Waldo Emerson

The independence of the master is based on the dependence of the slave.

Angela Davis

Neither slavery nor involuntary servitude, except as a punishment for crime whereof the party shall have been convicted, shall exist within the United States, or any place subject to their jurisdiction.

Thirteenth Amendment, U.S. Constitution, 1865

Socialism

The inherent vice of capitalism is the unequal sharing of blessings; the inherent virtue of socialism is the equal sharing of miseries.

Winston Churchill

Socialism is not at all the enemy of civilization. It only wants to extend civilization to all humanity; under capitalism, civilization is the monopoly of a privileged minority.

John Stuart Mill

What is constant in socialism boils down to the abolition of the exploitation of man by man.

Wladyslaw Gomulka

To be a Marxist does not mean that one becomes a Communist party member. There are as many varieties of Marxists as there are of Protestants.

Helen Foster Snow

Socialism is simply degenerate capitalism of bankrupt capitalists. Its one genuine object is to get more money for its professors.

H. L. Mencken

We should have had socialism already, but for the socialists.

George Bernard Shaw

We are all Socialists now-a-days.

Edward VII

I am a firm believer in socialism and I know that the quicker you have monopoly in this country the quicker you will have socialism.
Charles P. Steinmetz

Speeches

When a man is asked to make a speech, the first thing he has to decide is what to say.

Gerald Ford

All epoch-making revolutionary events have been produced not by written but by spoken word.

Adolf Hitler

Oratory is the power to talk people out of their sober and natural opinions.

Paul Chatfield

The man with power but without conscience, could, with an eloquent tongue . . . put this whole country into a flame.

Woodrow Wilson

Men use thought only to justify their wrongdoings and speech only to conceal their thoughts.

Voltaire

Rhetoric is the art of ruling the minds of men.

Plato

His speech was a fine sample, on the whole,
Of the rhetoric, which the learn'd call rigmarole.

Lord Byron

Speech is power: speech is to persuade, to convert, to compel.

Ralph Waldo Emerson

I sometimes marvel at the extraordinary docility with which Americans submit to speeches.

Adlai Stevenson

The object of oratory alone is not truth, but persuasion.

Thomas Macaulay

Why don't th' feller who says, "I'm not a speechmaker," let it go at that instead o' givin' a demonstration?

Kin Hubbard

The politicians were talking themselves red, white and blue in the face.

Clare Boothe Luce

The compulsion of politicians to talk too much is in our day a very big obstacle to accomplishing what they all say they want to do.

Walter Lippmann

My father gave me these hints on speech-making: "Be sincere, be brief . . . be seated."

James Roosevelt

The best orator is one who can make men see with their ears.

Arab saying

The Speaker's eye: the most elusive organ that Nature ever created.

Stanley Baldwin

Nothing is so unbelievable that oratory cannot make it acceptable.

Cicero

A democracy in effect is no more than an aristocracy of orators, interrupted sometimes with the temporary monarchy of one orator.

Thomas Hobbes

Taxes

And it came to pass in those days, that there went out a decree from Caesar Augustus, that all the world should be taxed.

Luke 2:1

Governments last as long as the over-taxed can defend themselves against the under-taxed.

Bernhard Berenson

Taxation without representation is tyranny.

James Otis

If Patrick Henry thought that taxation without representation was bad he should see how bad it is with representation.

Old Farmer's Almanac

Over-taxation is not an incident, but rather a principle.

Karl Marx

Do we imagine that our assessments operate equally? Nothing can be more contrary to the fact. Wherever a discretionary power is lodged in any set of men over the property of their neighbors, they will abuse it.

Alexander Hamilton

Tax reform means, "Don't tax you, don't tax me. Tax that fellow behind the tree."

Russell Long

Some taxpayers close their eyes, some stop their ears, some shut their mouths, but all pay through the nose.

Evan Esar

Where there is an income tax, the just man will pay more and the
unjust less on the same amount of income.

Plato

The thing generally raised on city land is taxes.

Charles Dudley Warner

To tax and to please, no more than to love and to be wise, is not
given to man.

Edmund Burke

Of all debts, men are least willing to pay taxes. What a satire is this
on government.

Ralph Waldo Emerson

Anybody has a right to evade taxes if he can get away with it. No
citizen has a moral obligation to assist in maintaining his government.

J. Pierpont Morgan

We are compelled to admire the efficiency of the government in
assessing and collecting taxes.

William Feather

Taxes are not levied for the benefit of the taxed.

Robert Heinlein

Taxes, after all, are the dues that we pay for the privileges of mem-
bership in an organized society.

Franklin D. Roosevelt

Taxes are what we pay for civilized society.

Oliver Wendell Holmes, Jr.

Blessed are the young, for they shall inherit the national debt.

Herbert Hoover

'Tis pleasant to observe, how free the present Age is in laying taxes
on the next.

Jonathan Swift

The income tax has made more liars out of the American people
than golf has.

Will Rogers

The hardest thing in the world to understand is the income tax.

Albert Einstein

There is something wrong with any law that causes that many people to have to take a whole day off their jobs to find out how to comply.

T. Coleman Andrews

Never will it be, that a people overlaid with taxes should ever become valiant and martial.

Francis Bacon

The power to tax involves the power to destroy.

John Marshall

Taxation under every form presents but a choice of evils.

David Ricardo

There is one difference between a tax collector and a taxidermist—the taxidermist leaves the hide.

Mortimer Caplan

The taxpayer—that's someone who works for the federal government but doesn't have to take a civil service examination.

Ronald Reagan

There is just one thing I can promise you about the outer-space program: your dollars will go farther.

Wernher von Braun

I've never believed that just cutting taxes alone will cause output and employment to expand.

David Stockman

But in this world, nothing is certain but death and taxes.

Benjamin Franklin

Trade

Free trade is not a principle; it is an expedient.

Benjamin Disraeli

The call for free trade is as unavailing as the cry of a spoiled child for the moon. It never has existed; it never will exist.

Henry Clay

If we will not buy we cannot sell.

William McKinley

In all the ancient states and empires those who had the shipping had the wealth.

William Petty

The produce of a country exchanges for the produce of other countries, at such values as are required in order that the whole of her exports may exactly pay for the whole of her imports.

John Stuart Mill

Sooner or later every war of trade becomes a war of blood.

Eugene V. Debs

A merchant may, perhaps, be a man of an enlarged mind, but there is nothing in trade connected with an enlarged mind.

Samuel Johnson

One of the purest fallacies is that trade follows the flag. Trade follows the lowest price current. . . . Trade knows no flag.

Andrew Carnegie

Transportation

The railroads are not run for the benefit of the dear public. That cry is nonsense. They are built for men who invest their money and expect to get a fair percentage on the same.

William H. Vanderbilt

The true history of the United States is the history of transportation . . . in which names of railroad presidents are more significant than those of Presidents of the United States.

Phillip Guedalla

California is proud to be the home of the freeway.

Ronald Reagan

Our national flower is the concrete cloverleaf.

Lewis Mumford

Calling a taxi in Texas is like calling a rabbi in Iraq.

Fran Lebowitz

Treason

I love treason but hate a traitor.

Julius Caesar

Treason doth never prosper: what's the reason? For if it prosper, none dare call it treason.

John Harington

I hate the idea of causes, and if I had to choose between betraying my country and betraying my friend, I hope I should have the guts to betray my country.

E. M. Forster

The issue between the Republicans and Democrats is clearly drawn. It has been deliberately drawn by those who have been in charge of twenty years of treason.

Joseph McCarthy

Treason against the United States shall consist only in levying war against them, or in adhering to their enemies, giving them aid and comfort.

Article III, U.S. Constitution, 1787

I know many have been taught to think that moderation, in a case like this, is a sort of treason.

Edmund Burke

Our whole history is treason; our blood was attainted before we were born; our creeds are infidelity to the mother church; our Constitution, treason to our fatherland.

Theodore Parker

Tyranny

The best government is a benevolent tyranny tempered by an occasional assassination.

Voltaire

A man may build himself a throne of bayonets, but he cannot sit on it.

William Ralph Inge

Tyrants are always assassinated too late; that is their great excuse.

E. M. Cioran

The tyranny of legislators is at present, and will be for many years, our most formidable danger. The tyranny of the executive will arise in its turn, but at a more distant period.

Thomas Jefferson

Bad laws are the worst sort of tyranny.

Edmund Burke

The worst tyranny is that of misapplied laws.

Metternich

Where law ends, tyranny begins.

William Pitt, the Elder

Tyrants seldom want pretexts.

Edmund Burke

Any excuse will serve a tyrant.

Aesop

Tyranny is always better organized than freedom.

Charles Péguy

Tyrants commonly cut off the stairs by which they climb into their thrones.

Thomas Fuller

All men would be tyrants if they could.

Daniel Defoe

Righteous vengefulness . . . has always made new tyrants out of aging liberations.

Erik Erikson

He who endeavors to control the mind is a tyrant, and he who submits is a slave.

Robert G. Ingersoll

For somehow this tyranny's disease, to trust no friends.

Aeschylus

The evils of tyranny are rarely seen but by him who resists it.

John Hay

Tyranny, like hell, is not easily conquered.

Thomas Paine

The mob is the mother of tyrants.

Dionysius

States decree the most illustrious rewards, not to him who catches the thief, but to him who kills a tyrant.

Aristotle

All executive power—from the reign of ancient kings to the rule of modern dictators—has the outward appearance of efficiency.

William O. Douglas

So long as men worship the Caesars and Napoleons, Caesars and Napoleons will duly rise and make them miserable.

Aldous Huxley

Vice-Presidency

The Vice-Presidency is sort of like the last cookie on the plate. Everybody insists he won't take it, but somebody always does.

Bill Vaughan

A spare tire on the automobile of government.

John Nance Garner

My country has contrived for me the most insignificant office that ever the invention of man contrived or his imagination conceived.

John Adams

Once there were two brothers: one ran away to sea, the other was elected Vice-President—and nothing was ever heard from either of them again.

Thomas Marshall

I have not been calling the signals. I have been in the position of a lineman doing some of the downfield blocking.

Hubert Humphrey

I am the first Eagle Scout vice president of the United States!

Gerald Ford

The Vice-Presidency of the United States isn't worth a pitcher of warm spit.

John Nance Garner

War

War is nothing more than the continuation of politics by other means.

Karl von Clausewitz

Thank goodness we don't live in medieval times when people fought wars over ideas.

Wojciech Jaruzelski

There is a boy here today who looks on war as all glory, but boys, it is all hell.

William T. Sherman

The more I study the world, the more I am convinced of the inability of brute force to create anything durable.

Napoleon Bonaparte

You can't say that civilizations don't advance, for in every war they kill you in a new way.

Will Rogers

Out of this war [Vietnam] are going to come some of the finest people this country has seen.

William Westmoreland

The true lesson of the Vietnam war is: certainty of purpose and ruthlessness of execution win wars.

Ronald Reagan

The belief in the possibility of a short, decisive war appears to be one of the most ancient and dangerous of human illusions.

Robert Lynd

In the midst of the most destructive foreign war ... the greater part of manufacturers may frequently flourish greatly; and on the contrary, they may decline on the return to peace.

Adam Smith

Profits are springing, like weeds, from the fields of the dead.

Rosa Luxemburg

Instead of the government taking over industry when the war broke out, industry took over the government.

Claire Gillis

The success of war is not so much dependent on arms, as on the possession of money.

Thucydides

There is no nation on earth so dangerous as a nation fully armed, and bankrupt at home.

Henry Cabot Lodge

To destroy is still the strongest instinct of our nature.

Max Beerbohm

Is war a biological necessity? As regards the earliest cultures the answer is emphatically negative.

Bronislaw Malinowski

War, like any other racket, pays high dividends to the very few.... The cost of operations is always transferred to the people who do not profit.

Smedley Butler

War in its fairest form implies a perpetual violation of humanity and justice.

Edward Gibbon

Never think that war, no matter how necessary, nor how justified, is not a crime.

Ernest Hemingway

Laws are inoperative in war.

Cicero

Force, and fraud, are in war the two cardinal virtues.

John Milton

Wars are just to those for whom they are necessary.

Edmund Burke

The clatter of arms drowns the voice of law.

M. E. Montaigne

All oppression creates a state of war.

Simone de Beauvoir

Battle, n. A method of untying with the teeth a political knot that would not yield to the tongue.

Ambrose Bierce

Militarism is a fever for conquest, with peace for a shield, using music and brass buttons to dazzle and divert the populace.

Elbert Hubbard

As long as there are sovereign nations possessing great power, war is inevitable.

Albert Einstein

War is the father and king of all: some he has made gods, and some men; some slaves, and some free.

Heraclitus

War makes the victors stupid and the vanquished vengeful.

Friedrich Nietzsche

War hath no fury like a noncombatant.

M. E. Montaigne

For what can war but endless war still breed?

John Milton

We must conquer war, or war will conquer us.

Ely Culbertson

In time of war the first casualty is truth.

Boake Carter

We are going to have peace even if we have to fight for it.

Dwight D. Eisenhower

We don't declare war anymore; we declare national defense.

Eugene McCarthy

War is not healthy for children and other living things.

Antiwar poster, 1967

You always write it's bombing, bombing, bombing. It's not bombing. It's air support.

H. E. Opfer

All wars are popular for the first thirty days.

Arthur Schlesinger, Jr.

Wars have never hurt anybody except the people who die.

Salvador Dali

Everyone may begin a war at his pleasure, but cannot so finish it.

Niccolò Machiavelli

They told me it would disrupt my life less if I got killed.

Joseph Heller

No protracted war can fail to endanger the freedom of a democratic country.

Alexis de Tocqueville

We flattened cities in Germany and Japan in World War II. I don't know what's so sacred about Hanoi. . . . Let world opinion go fly a kite.

Mendel Rivers

The only thing that's been a worse flop than the organization of nonviolence has been the organization of violence.

Joan Baez

The end move in politics is always to pick up a gun.

Buckminster Fuller

The basic problems facing the world today are not susceptible to a military solution.

John F. Kennedy

I bomb, therefore I am.

Philip Slater

The grim fact is that we prepare for war like precocious giants and for peace like retarded pygmies.

Lester B. Pearson

You can no more win a war than you can win an earthquake.

Jeannette Rankin

I cannot believe that war is the best solution. No one won the last war, and no one will win the next war.

Eleanor Roosevelt

Another such victory and we are ruined.

Pyrrhus

They there may dig each other's graves,
And call the sad work glory.

Percy Bysshe Shelley

It is well that war is so terrible—we would grow too fond of it.

Robert E. Lee

No one is so foolish as to prefer war to peace, in which, instead of sons burying fathers, fathers bury their sons.

Herodotus

War . . . is a relation, not between man and man, but between State and State, and individuals are enemies only accidently, not as men, nor even as citizens, but as soldiers. .

C. S. Montesquieu

There is no human activity that stands in such constant and universal contact with chance as does war.

Karl von Clausewitz

What is the use of physicians like myself trying to help parents to bring up children healthy and happy, to have them killed in such numbers for a cause that is ignoble?

Benjamin Spock

When women have a voice in national and international affairs, war will cease forever.

Augusta Stowe-Gullen

It would be genuine revolution if women would suddenly stop loving the victors in violent encounters.

Germaine Greer

Very little is known about the War of 1812 because the Americans lost it.

Eric Nicol

Woe to the statesman who does not find a reason for war that will hold water when the war is over.

Otto von Bismarck

This war, like the next war, is a war to end war.

David Lloyd George

Wealth

Prosperity of the middling and lower orders depends upon the fortunes and light taxes of the rich.

Andrew Mellon

We can have democracy in this country or we can have great wealth concentrated in the hands of a few, but we can't have both.

Louis D. Brandeis

If you pick up a starving dog and make him prosperous, he will not bite you. This is the principal difference between a man and a dog.

Mark Twain

If we made an income pyramid out of a child's blocks, with each layer portraying $1,000 of income, the peak would be far higher than the Eiffel Tower, but almost all of us would be within a yard of the ground.

Paul Samuelson

People of privilege will always risk their complete destruction rather than surrender any material part of their advantage.

John Kenneth Galbraith

The rich never feel so good as when they are speaking of their possessions as responsibilities.

Robert Lynd

Nothing is more admirable than the fortitude with which millionaires tolerate the disadvantages of their wealth.

Rex Stout

Only the rich preach content to the poor.

Holbrook Jackson

The Irish famine of 1846 killed more than a million people, but it killed poor devils only. To the wealth of the country it did not the slightest damage.

Karl Marx

We must have a political state powerful enough to deal with corporate wealth, but how are we going to keep that state with its augmenting power from being captured by the force we want it to control?

Vernon Louis Parrington

It is to be regretted that the rich and powerful too often bend the acts of government to their selfish purposes.

Andrew Jackson

The people came to realize that wealth is not the fruit of labor but the result of organized protected robbery.

Frantz Fanon

The rich, in particular, are necessarily interested to support that order of things which can alone secure them in the possession of their own advantages.

Adam Smith

Wealth is a power usurped by the few to compel the many to labor for their benefit.

Percy Bysshe Shelley

[Wealth] The savings of many in the hands of one.

Eugene V. Debs

The ways to enrich are many, and most of them are foul.

Francis Bacon

If I keep my good character, I shall be rich enough.

Plato

I'm opposed to millionaires, but it would be dangerous to offer me the position.

Mark Twain

He has not acquired a fortune; the fortune has acquired him.

Bion

Failure seems to be regarded as the one unpardonable crime, success as the all-redeeming virtue, the acquisition of wealth as the single worthy aim of life.

Charles Francis Adams

Luxury and avarice—these pests have been the ruin of every state.

Cato

There are only two families in the world, my old grandmother used to say, the Haves and the Have-Nots.

Miguel de Cervantes

The hopes of the Republic cannot forever tolerate either unde-served poverty or self-serving wealth.

Franklin D. Roosevelt

When wealth is centralized the people are dispersed; when wealth is distributed the people are brought together.

Confucius

Work

When a man tells you he got rich through hard work, ask him *whose?*

Don Marquis

A Darwinian nation of economic fitness abhors idleness, dependence, nonproductivity.

Simone de Beauvoir

If one defines "dropout" to mean a person who has given up serious effort to meet his responsibilities, then every business office, government agency, golf club and university faculty would yield its quota.

John Gardner

It very seldom happens to a man that his business is his pleasure.

Samuel Johnson

There is dignity in work only when it is work freely accepted.

Albert Camus

It is not enough to be busy . . . the question is: what are we busy about?

Henry David Thoreau

The man who gives me employment, which I must have or suffer, that man is my master, let me call him what I will.

Henry George

More and more university students are convinced that work in

American society is morally empty, aesthetically ugly, and, under conditions of automation, economically unnecessary.

Michael Harrington

Lo! Men have become the tools of their tools.

Henry David Thoreau

The danger of the past was that men became slaves. The danger of the future is that men may become robots.

Erich Fromm

Work spares us from three great evils: boredom, vice and need.

Voltaire

Work is a necessity for man. Man invented the alarm clock.

Pablo Picasso

An unemployed existence is a worse negation of life than death itself. Because to live means to have something definite to do. . . .

José Ortega y Gasset

It [unemployment insurance] provides prepaid vacations for a segment of our country which has made it a way of life.

Ronald Reagan

Subject Index

Authors Index

(Rum.-born) bridge expert, 238

Cummings, Edward Estlin (1894–1962), Am. poet; painter, 107

Curzon, George Nathaniel (1859–1925), Eng. statesman, 153

Daladier, Edouard (1884–1970), Fr. statesman, 140

Daley, Richard Joseph (1902–1976), Chicago mayor, 135, 159

Dali, Salvador (1904–   ), Span. painter, 239

Dana, Charles Anderson (1819–1897), Am. journalist, 132

Dark, Alvin Ralph (1922–   ), Am. baseball manager, 26

Darrow, Clarence Seward (1857–1937), Am. lawyer, 82, 111, 181

Davies, John (1569–1626), Eng. judge; poet, 194

Davis, Adelle (1904–1973), Am. nutritionist, 96

Davis, Angela Yvonne (1944–   ), Am. civil rights activist; educ., 53, 221

Dawes, Charles Gates (1865–1951), U.S. v.-pres.; financier, 51

Debs, Eugene Victor (1885–1926), Am. Socialist leader, 53, 80, 114, 129, 229, 243

Decatur, Stephen (1779–1820), Am. naval officer, 161

Defoe, Daniel (1659?–1731), Eng. nov., 112, 118, 234

De Gaulle, Charles André Joseph Marie (1890–1970), Fr. gen.; pres., 54, 120, 169, 183

Demosthenes (385?–322 B.C.), Greek orator; statesman, 51

Devine, Edward Thomas (1867–1948), Am. sociol., 22

Dewey, John (1859–1952), Am. philos.; educ., 167

Diaz, José de la Cruz Porfirio (1830–1915), Mex. gen.; pres., 103

Dicey, Albert Venn (1835–1922), Eng. judge, 192

Dickens, Charles John Huffman (1812–1870), Eng. nov., 86

Diderot, Denis (1713–1784), Fr. encyclopedist, 75

Diogenes (412?–323 B.C.), Greek philos., 59

Dionysius (430?–?367 B.C.), Greek tyrant of Syracuse, 180, 234

Disraeli, Benjamin (1804–1881), Brit. prime min., 13, 32, 54, 61, 96, 120, 130, 159, 160, 172, 173, 216, 229

Douglas, Norman (1868–1952), Eng. author, 1

Douglas, William Orville (1898–1980), U.S. Supreme Court justice, 89, 179, 234

Douglass, Frederick (1817?–1895), Am. abolitionist, 83

Dreiser, Theodore (1871–1945), Am. nov.; editor, 7

Drucker, Peter Ferdinand (1909–   ), Am. writer; management consultant, 18, 57, 58, 70, 115

Drummond, Hugh (contemp.), pseud. for Am. psychiatrist

Dryden, John (1631–1700), Eng. poet; dram., 36

Du Bois, William Edward Burghardt (1868–1963), Am. educ.; writer, 176

Dubos, René Jules (1901–1981), Fr. bacteriol., 70

Duckett, Hansell B. (n.d.), 88

Dudley, Charles Edward (1780–1841), Am. polit., 172

Dulles, John Foster (1888–1959), Am. diplomat, 156

Dumas, Alexandre, fils (1824–1895), Fr. nov.; dram., 176

Dunne, Finley Peter (1867–1936), Am. humorist, 18, 74, 111

Durant, Ariel (1898–1981), Am. hist., 48, 215

Durant, William James (1885–1981), Am. hist., 48, 108, 215

Dzhugashvili, Iosif Vissarionovich (1879–1953), Russ. Communist leader, 59

Eban, Abba (1915–   ), Israel (S. African-born) polit., 185